A Guide to Professional Organizations for Teachers of Language and Literature in the United States and Canada

COMPILED BY

Adrienne Marie Ward

The Modern Language Association of America
New York, 1990

Copyright © 1990 by The Modern Language Association of America

Library of Congress Cataloging-in-Publication Data

Ward, Adrienne Marie, 1964–
    A guide to professional organizations for teachers of language and
literature in the United States and Canada / compiled by Adrienne
Marie Ward. — 2nd ed.
        p.   cm.
    ISBN 0-87352-196-X
    1. Philology—Societies, etc.—Directories. 2. Philology—Study and
teaching—United States—Directories. 3. Philology—Study and teaching
—Canada—Directories. I. Title.
P11.W36   1990
418'.007'073—dc20   90-31194

Published by The Modern Language Association of America
10 Astor Place, New York, New York 10003-6981

Contents

Preface

This expanded, second edition of *A Guide to Professional Organizations in the United States and Canada for Teachers of Language and Literature* reflects changes in the needs and interests of teachers of language and literature and in the profession as a whole over the past ten years. The groups listed can no longer be classified strictly as professional organizations for teachers of language and literature but now comprise a variety of membership associations, including those concerned with ethnicity, period studies, political issues, technology, interdisciplinary study, and languages and literatures other than European.

The *Guide* provides essential information on 214 professional organizations and societies. All the allied organizations of the Modern Language Association, the humanities organizations in the American Council of Learned Societies, and the organizations listed as sponsoring organizations in the *MLA Directory of Periodicals* (1988) were surveyed in the summer and fall of 1988. Respondents were given the opportunity during the summer of 1989 to verify and modify the descriptive statements. The *Guide* does not evaluate information supplied by the respondents; instead, it offers readers the opportunity to form their own judgments.

The main body of the *Guide* contains 133 listings for associations. The entries are arranged alphabetically and numbered consecutively. Each entry lists the organization's name, acronym, address, year founded, size, phone number, the title and name of the contact person at the organization, and its statement of purpose. The rest of the entry gives information about periodicals and books published, meetings, job placement services, prizes and fellowships awarded, programs and seminars sponsored, commissions, legislative efforts, and other activities.

The second section of the *Guide* lists eighty-one author societies, providing the year founded, title and name of the contact person at the organization, address, and size. Entries are arranged alphabetically by author. Cross-references are given when the name of the society does not contain that of the author.

A checklist of abbreviations follows the listings and includes several important scholarly organizations cited in the text but not given separate entries. The *Guide* concludes with a subject index; references are by entry number.

Readers seeking information concerning other organizations in the United States might wish to consult Gale Research Press's *Encyclopedia of Associations 1989* and, for information concerning those abroad, Gale's *International Organizations 1989.* The annual *Humanities Computing Yearbook,* published by Clarendon House, lists humanities computing organizations in the United States, Canada, and Great Britain. The annual *HEP Higher Education Directory,* published by Higher Education Publications, lists the addresses of higher education associations and education consortia in the United States.

We hope to update the data in the *Guide* regularly. We also hope to cover additional associations in future editions, and we invite readers to suggest names of organizations of interest to teachers of language and literature.

I would like to thank the many persons who responded to my requests for information and to express my appreciation to Walter S. Achtert, Judith Altreuter, Elizabeth Holland, Rebecca Hunsicker, and Joseph Gibaldi for their invaluable assistance.

AMW

Listing of
Professional Organizations

1. **Administrators and Teachers in English as a Second Language (ATESL)**
   1860 19th Street, NW
   Washington, DC 20009
Founded 1964
1,200 members
Tel. 202 462-4811
Staff Liaison: Colin Davies
ATESL is one of the professional-interest sections within the National Association for Foreign Student Affairs (see NAFSA). Its purposes are to promote quality instruction and services for international students in ESL by offering resources and professional development opportunities for teachers and administrators; to promote professionalism in the administrative and instructional aspects of ESL; to assemble, exchange, and distribute information on administration, research, and teaching concerned with ESL; to establish liaison's with other groups whose members have the same or similar professional interests; and to promote interest in and knowledge of the field of ESL in the wider community.

Publications
The Administration of Intensive English Language Programs. 1982.
Foreign Teaching Assistants in U.S. Universities. 1984.
Teaching English as a Second Language: A Guide for the Volunteer Teacher. 1986.
Teaching across Cultures in the University ESL Program. 1986.
Evaluation of the English Languages and Personnel. Forthcoming.
Testing and Evaluation of English Language Proficiency. Forthcoming.

The association meets at NAFSA's annual conference. The twelve regional groups of NAFSA each hold an annual conference and occasional workshops.
   1990: 15–18 May, Portland, OR
   1991: 24–27 May, Boston, MA
   1992: 23–26 May, Chicago, IL

NAFSA issues a monthly *Job Bulletin* that includes ESL positions, and it organizes a Job Search Office at its annual conferences. It also holds a bimonthly employment roundtable at its Washington, DC, headquarters.

Through the NAFSA Field Service, ATESL provides experienced consultants to institutions of higher learning regarding ESL programs for foreign students.

2. **African Activist Association**
   James S. Coleman African Studies Center
   10244 Bunche Hall
   University of California, Los Angeles
   Los Angeles, CA 90024
Founded 1969
Tel. 213 825-3686
The African Activist Association serves as a progressive forum for discourse, criticism, and activism around local and international issues relating to Africa. The association seeks to encourage greater knowledge and understanding of the long historic traditions of the African people, their struggle for liberation, and their links to other oppressed peoples of the world. Although primarily composed of

UCLA students, the association encourages staff and faculty members of UCLA and residents of Los Angeles to join.

UFAHAMU, named after the Swahili word for comprehension and understanding, is an interdisciplinary journal representing strong and committed views on Africa and addressing both the general reader and the scholar. It is published three times a year.

3.   **African Literature Association (ALA)**
       Africana Studies and Research Center
       Cornell University
       310 Triphammer Road
       Ithaca, NY 14850
Founded 1974
550 members
Tel. 607 255-0534
President: Anne Adams

ALA is an independent professional society open to scholars, teachers and writers from every country. It exists primarily to help a worldwide audience appreciate the efforts of African writers and artists. As an organization, ALS affirms the primacy of the African peoples in shaping the future of African literature and actively supports the African peoples in their struggle for liberation.

Periodicals

Research in African Literatures. Ed. Richard Bjornson (Center for Comparative Study, Ohio State Univ., Columbus, OH 43210). Quarterly.
ALA Bulletin. Ed. Stephen Arnold (Dept. of Comparative Literature, Univ. of Alberta, Edmonton, AB T6G 2EG). Quarterly.
Selected Annual ALA Conference Papers.

In March 1989, for the first time, ALA held its annual conference in Dakar, Senegal. The 1990 meeting will take place 4–7 April, in Madison, WI. The special topic will be Tongue and Mother Tongue: African Literature and the Perpetual Search for Identity.

4.   **African Studies Association (ASA)**
       Emory University
       Credit Union Building
       Atlanta, GA 30322
Founded 1957
Tel. 404 329-6410
Executive Secretary: Edna Bay

ASA was founded to bring together persons with scholarly and professional interests in Africa, to provide useful services to the Africanist community, and to publish and distribute scholarly Africanist materials.

Periodicals

African Studies Review. Ed. Carol B. Thompson. Pub. 3 times a year. Articles of scholarly and bibliographical interest.
ASA News. Ed. Edna G. Bay. Quarterly. News, opinion editorials, and correspondence.

Issue: A Journal of Opinion. Ed. Harvey Glickman. Semiannual. Timely comment on events in Africa and African studies.
History in Africa. Ed. David Henige. Annual. Studies and analyses of African history.

The association's Crossroads Press publishes scholarly and bibliographical materials related to the Third World, a traditional-medicine series, a basic Africana series, and directories on African and Third World research and scholars.

Meeting: 1990: Baltimore, MD

ASA's Herskovits Award honors the author of a distinguished scholarly work on Africa.

5.   American Academy of Religion (AAR)
Syracuse University
501 Hall of Languages
Syracuse, NY 13244-1170
Founded 1909
5,600 members
Tel. 315 443-4019; FAX 315 443-5390
Executive Director and Treasurer: James B. Wiggins
The academy aims to stimulate scholarship and foster research in the field of religious studies.

Periodicals
Critical Review of Books. Annual.
Journal of the American Academy of Religion. Quarterly.
Religious Studies News. Pub. 5 times a year. Pub. in association with the Society of Biblical Literature (see SBL).
Openings. Bimonthly placement assistance service. Pub. in association with SBL.

Selected Publications, 1988
The Paradox of Intention: Reaching the Goal by Giving Up the Attempt to Reach It. By Marvin C. Shaw. Studies in Religion.
Recovering the Personal: Religious Language and the Postcritical Quest of H. Richard Niebuhr. By R. Melvin Keiser. Studies in Religion.
John Calvin's Perspectival Anthropology. By Mary Potter Engel. Academy Series.
Comprehending the Guru: Toward a Grammar of Religious Perception. By Daniel Gold. Academy Series.
Black Womanist Ethics. By Katie G. Cannon. Academy Series.

AAR convenes jointly with SBL.
1990: 17–20 Nov., New Orleans, LA
1991: 23–26 Nov., Kansas City, MO

The academy sponsors Awards for Excellence in Books of Religion to provide formal recognition of works of distinctive originality, intelligence, and creativity that decisively affect the way religion is understood and interpreted. AAR annually awards research grants in support of individual and collaborative projects.

AAR is a constituent member of ACLS, NHA, and the National Council on Religion in Public Education.

6.   American Anthropological Association (AAA)
1703 New Hampshire Avenue, NW
Washington, DC 20009
Founded 1902
10,400 members
Tel. 202 232-8800
Director of Information Services: David B. Givens
AAA is the world's largest organization of individuals interested in anthropology. Its purposes are to encourage scholarly and professional communication among anthropologists and to encourage public understanding of anthropology. While the association represents the field as a whole, its twenty-two constituent units represent various subfields and regional organizations. Those units of interest to teachers of language and literature include the American Ethnological Society, Archaeological Section, and the societies for Cultural Anthropology, Latin American Anthropology, Linguistic Anthropology, Psychological Anthropology, Urban Anthropology, and Visual Anthropology.

Members receive the *Anthropology Newsletter*, published nine times a year, and the particular journals, newsletters or other publications of the constituent units they join. These include *American Ethnologist, American Anthropologist, Anthropology and Education Quarterly, Cultural Anthropology, Anthropology and Humanism Quarterly, Ethos*, and *City and Society*. AAA also publishes an annual *Guide to Departments of Anthropology*.

Publications
Anthropology and Public Policy: A Dialogue. Ed. Walter Goldschmidt. 1986.
Honor and Shame in the Unity of the Mediterranean. By David D. Gilmore. 1987.
Handbook on Ethical Issues in Anthropology. By J. Cassell and S. E. Jacobs. 1987.
Anthropology for Tomorrow: Creating Practitioner-Oriented Applied Anthropology Programs.
    Ed. Robert T. Trotter II. 1988.

The association convenes an annual meeting lasting 4–5 days. At this time members of the association and its constituent units hold business meetings, present awards, read scientific papers, and discuss topics of importance to anthropology. The 1990 meeting will take place 28 November–2 December in New Orleans, LA.

The association operates a placement service and sponsors workshops and a two-day job clinic each year.

AAA is a constituent society of ACLS.

7.   American Antiquarian Society (AAS)
185 Salisbury Street
Worcester, MA 01609
Founded 1812
522 members
Tel. 508 755-5221
Director and Librarian: Marcus A. McCorison
AAS promotes research and provides educational opportunities pertaining to the history and culture of the United States and Canada through 1876. The society

maintains a major research library and offers research and educational programs based on its library collections.

Periodicals

Proceedings of the American Antiquarian Society. Ed. John B. Hench. Pub. Apr. and Oct.
Newsletter of the AAS. Ed. Lynnette P. Sodha. Semiannual.
The Book: Newsletter of the Program in the History of the Book. Ed. John B. Hench. Pub. Mar., July, and Nov.

AAS publishes scholarly monographs, bibliographies, and facsimile editions. Recent titles include Roger Collegehartier's *Frenchness in the History of the Book: From the History of Publishing to the History of Reading* (1987) and Hannah D. French's *Bookbinding in Early America: Seven Essays on Masters and Methods* (1986).

The annual meeting is held on the third Wednesday of October in Worcester, MA; the semiannual meeting is held in another city on the third Wednesday of April.

To encourage imaginative and productive research in its extensive library collections in early American history and culture, AAS awards short- and long-term visiting research fellowships in association with the National Endowment for the Humanities, NEMLA, ASECS, and the Newberry Library.

The North American Imprints Program (NAIP) is a long-term undertaking to construct detailed, computerized bibliographic records of all North American imprints.
  The Program in the History of the Book comprises scholarly activities, including annual lectures, workshops, seminars, conferences, publications, and residential fellowships. Areas of inquiry include publishing history; the distribution of printed works to readers; and the influence of books, pamphlets, newspapers, and graphic-arts materials on American culture.

AAS is a charter member of ACLS and the Independent Libraries Association.

8.   American Association for Adult and Continuing Education (AAACE)

1112 16th Street, NW
Washington, DC 20036
Founded 1982
3,400 members
Tel. 202 463-6333
Executive Director: Judith Ann Koloski

AAACE is an international professional association whose mission is to unify the profession; to advocate adult education to legislators and the public; to promote research; to provide professional opportunities through conferences, seminars, and workshops on a national and local level; and to distribute information through newsletters, books, pamphlets, and reports.

Periodicals

Adult Learning. Ed. Jeanette E. Smith. Pub. 8 times a year.
Adult Education Quarterly. Ed. Ronald Cervero and Sharon Morriam. Research in the field.
Online. Pub. 10 times a year. Newsletter.

Meetings
>1990: 5–11 Nov., Salt Lake City, UT
>1991: 13–19 Nov., Montréal, PQ

AAACE sponsors a Speakers Bureau and job referral service.

9.   American Association for Applied Linguistics (AAAL)
>Suite 211, 1325 18th Street, NW
>Washington, DC 20036-6501

Founded 1977
500 members
Tel. 202 835-1714
Secretary: Paul Angelis
AAAL is a professional organization of scholars who are interested in and actively contributing to the field of applied linguistics. The association promotes research, facilitates the distribution and exchange of information, and organizes scholarly conferences and meetings.

AAAL's newsletter, edited by Conna Christian and published three times a year, includes membership lists, preliminary programs of annual meetings, publication notices, conference reports, and brief articles. The association jointly sponsors the journal *Applied Linguistics* with the British Association for Applied Linguistics.

AAAL cooperates in producing publications, such as the *International Directory of Applied Linguistics Organizations*, with the Center for Applied Linguistics.

The association holds an annual conference in conjunction with the Linguistic Society of America (see LSA).

AAAL awards a prize for the best paper presented by a graduate student at the annual meeting.

The association is the American affiliate of the International Association of Applied Linguistics (AILA).

10.   American Association for the Advancement of Slavic Studies (AAASS)
>128 Encina Commons
>Stanford University
>Stanford, CA 94305-6029

Founded 1948
3,500 members
Tel. 415 723-9668
Executive Director: Dorothy Atkinson
The association's goal is the advancement of Slavic studies, including the study of all Soviet and East European languages and literatures.

Periodicals
Slavic Review: American Quarterly of Soviet and East European Studies. Ed. Sidney Monas
>(Box 8180, Univ. of Texas, Austin, TX 78713-8180).

American Bibliography of Slavic and East European Studies. Ed. Barbara Dash. Annual.
AAASS Newsletter. Ed. Andreas Argyres. Pub. 5 times a year. Includes listings of
    employment opportunities.

Meetings
        1990: 18–21 Oct., Washington, DC
        1991: 22–25 Nov., Miami, FL

The Vucinich Prize is awarded annually for humanistic studies in the Soviet-East
European field.

AAASS has committees on language training and, with the American Council
of Teachers of Russian (see ACTR) and the American Association of Teachers
of Slavic and East European Languages (see AATSEEL), a committee on college
and precollege relations.

    AAASS is affiliated with the International Committee for Soviet and East Eu-
ropean Studies and is a constituent member of ACLS.

11.   American Association of Australian Literary Studies (AAALS)
        The Edward A. Clark Center for Australian Studies
        Harry Ransom Humanities Research Center
        Austin, TX 78713-7219
Founded 1985
120 members
Tel. 512 471-7219
President: Robert Ross
AAALS aims to encourage the study of Australian literature in North American
universities and schools, to provide materials for that study, to inform the general
public about Australian literature, to offer a forum for communication among
North Americans interested in Australian literature, to form links with scholars
abroad, and to promote the kind of cultural exchange that leads to international
understanding.

Periodicals
Antipodes. Ed. Robert Ross. Semiannual. Each issue focuses on a theme or area
        of interest in Australian literature; the spring issue features a bibliography
        of Australian literature and scholarly criticism.
AALS Newsletter. Ed. Carolyn Bliss (1453 E. 8020 South, Sandy, UT 84093). Semi-
        annual.

The association has published a pamphlet, edited by Alexandra Cromwell: *From
Outback to City: Changing Preoccupations in Australian Literature of the Twentieth Century*
(1988).

AAALS sponsors an annual spring conference, as well as informal meetings at
the MLA convention and at the meetings of other scholarly associations. The
next conference will be held 4–7 April 1990 at Rollins College, Winterpark, FL.
Peter Carey will deliver the keynote address.

12.   American Association of Professors of Yiddish (AAPY)
NSF 350
Queen's College
Flushing, NY 11367
Founded 1972
175 members
Tel. 718 520-7067
Secretary: Joseph C. Landis
AAPY is the professional association of teachers of Yiddish in American universities. Through its Conference on Modern Jewish Studies, the association promotes scholarship in related literatures, such as Jewish American, Jewish German, Jewish French, Jewish Spanish, and Hebrew. Membership is open to anyone who teaches Yiddish language and literature, including Yiddish literature in translation.

Periodicals
Yiddish (including *Modern Jewish Studies Annual*). Ed. Joseph C. Landis. Quarterly.
AAPY-MJS Newsletter. Ed. Joseph C. Landis. Irregular.

Publications
Sidor Belarsky Yiddish Songbook. 1988.
Aspects of I. B. Singer. Ed. Joseph C. Landis. 1986.
Memoirs of the Yiddish Stage. Ed. Joseph C. Landis. 1984.

AAPY meets annually at the MLA convention. Topics at the 1990 convention will include Modern Yiddish Literature at 125: Studies and Assessments and The Jewish Writer in a Changing America: Roth and Kosinski.

AAPY is an allied organization of the MLA.

13.   American Association of Teachers of Arabic (AATA)
Johns Hopkins University — SAIS
1619 Massachusetts Avenue, NW
Washington, DC 20036
Founded 1965
230 members
Tel. 202 663-5750
Executive Director: Gerald E. Lampe
The association promotes high standards of scholarship in Arabic studies and facilitates communication among scholars through meetings and publications. AATA maintains liaisons with scholars in Arab universities to keep abreast of developments in their Arabic language and teaching programs. Members include teachers of Arabic subjects — the language, literature, linguistics, and culture — and other people with a keen interest in such studies.

Periodicals
Al-Arabiyya. Ed. Frederic J. Cadora and Michael Cadora (Dept. of Judaic and
    Near-Eastern Languages and Literatures, Ohio State Univ., Columbus,
    OH 43210). Annual.
AATA Newsletter. Pub. 3 times a year.

Several workshops, set up under the auspices of AATA, led to the development and publication of two textbooks: one, a revised edition of the major textbook used in teaching Arabic as a second language in the United States, Canada, and the Arab world, *Elementary Modern Standard Arabic*, by P. Abboud et al. (Ann Arbor: Univ. of Michigan, 1975); and the other, a textbook for the teaching of intermediate Arabic, *Intermediate Modern Standard Arabic*, P. Abboud et al. (Ann Arbor: Univ. of Michigan, 1971). The association has also developed an Arabic proficiency exam.

AATA holds an annual meeting in conjunction with the Middle East Studies Association of North America (see MESA). The 1990 meeting will be held 10–13 November in San Antonio, TX.

AATA conducts an annual Arabic Translation Contest.

AATA is a member of JNCL/CLOIS.

14. American Association of Teachers of Esperanto (Amerika Asocio de Instruistoj de Esperanto) (AATE/AAIE)
     4710 Dexter Drive, No. 3
     Santa Barbara, CA 93110-1325
Founded 1962
93 members
Tel. 805 967-5241
Secretary: Dorothy Holland-Kaupp
The association promotes cooperative action by teachers to introduce Esperanto into all kinds of schools, to make possible the application of Esperanto by students and instructors through correspondence and visits, to share pedagogical information through Esperanto, and to facilitate personal and material exchanges among teachers, across the lines of nationality, race, sex, religion, politics, or language.

Periodical: *Quarterly Bulletin*. Ed. Dorothy Holland-Kaupp. Covers pedagogy and application of teaching techniques to Esperanto; lists Esperanto classes in the United States and abroad and names and addresses of Esperantists who want to correspond.

AATE convenes annually the last week in July.

The association encourages participation in a three-week summer program, with courses on four levels, at San Francisco State University. This program features total immersion in the language, and AATE offers promising Esperantists scholarships to attend. (Write Cathy Schulze, 410 Darrell Rd., Hillsborough, CA 94010.)

AATE is affiliated with the International League of Teachers of Esperanto and is an allied organization of the MLA.

15. American Association of Teachers of French (AATF)
     57 East Armory Avenue
     Champaign, IL 61820
Founded 1927
11,000 members
Tel. 217 333-2842
Executive Director: Fred M. Jenkins

The purpose of AATF, according to its Constitution, is "to represent the French language in North America and to encourage dissemination, both in the schools and in the general public, of knowledge concerning all aspects of the culture and civilization of France and the French-speaking world." The association supports projects designed to advance French language and literature and promotes reciprocal communication among French teachers at all levels.

Periodicals

The French Review. Ed. Ronald W. Tobin (Dept. of French and Italian, Univ. of California, Santa Barbara, CA 93106). Pub. 6 times a year.

AATF National Bulletin. Ed. Jane Black Goepper (431 Collins Ave., Cincinnati, OH 45202). Quarterly newsletter.

Meetings are held both in the United States and abroad.
> 1990: 2–5 July, New Orleans, LA
> 1991: July, Minneapolis, MN
> 1992: July, Strasbourg, France

AATF sponsors a placement bureau for teachers and professors of French.

The National French Contest, an annual competition for students of French at the elementary and secondary school levels, enrolled 81,000 participants in 1987–88. The top prizes include study trips to Quebec. (Write Sidney L. Teitelbaum, Box 86, Plainview, NY 11803.) AATF annually awards fifty summer scholarships for study in France, Quebec, and Africa. The cultural services of the French embassy fund thirty-five scholarships for study in France, and the government of Quebec funds fifteen scholarships for study at Laval University in Quebec. The Société Honoraire de Français for outstanding American students of French at the high school level has four hundred active chapters in American schools; it awards scholarships, study trips, and other prizes. (Write Stephen Foster, Dept. of Foreign Languages, Old Dominion Univ., Norfolk, VA 23508.)

AATF sponsors a traveling realia exhibit for classes and French clubs. (Write to Evelyn Vandiver, 2246 Cumberland Ave., Charlotte, NC 28203.) The Bureau de Correspondance Scolaire, a pen-pal agency, matches American students of French at the high school and junior high school levels with students of English in France and pairs American classes with classes in France for group correspondence. The Pedagogical Aids Bureau offers teaching aids such as maps, postcards, and other articles at reasonable prices.

AATF maintains permanent commissions in areas of interest to its members, under the following headings: Exchange of Pedagogical Materials with France and Québec (MOPED); FLES/FLEX/Immersion Programs; and Professional Standards.

AATF is a member of NFMLTA.

16.   American Association of Teachers of German (AATG)
112 Haddontowne Court, No. 104
Cherry Hill, NJ 08034
Founded 1926
6,500 members
Tel. 609 795-9398; FAX 609 795-5553

Executive Director: Helene Zimmer-Loew

AATG is dedicated to the advancement and improvement of the teaching of the language, literature, and culture of the German-speaking countries. The association's long-range plan, adopted in 1987, seeks to improve the quality of German instruction at all levels; increase German enrollments in American schools and colleges; improve relations with other organizations with similar interests, such as in the legislative support of language and international studies and the teaching and evaluation of language study; and promote research in the German language, literature, and culture as well as in foreign language learning and teaching in general. Membership in AATG automatically makes one a member of one of the sixty-two local chapters.

Periodicals

The German Quarterly. Ed. Paul Michael Lützler (German Dept., Washington Univ., St. Louis, MO 63130). Literary and philological scholarship.

Die Unterrichtspraxis. Ed. George F. Peters (A-615 Well Hall, Michigan State Univ., East Lansing, MI 48824-1027). Semiannual. Pedagogy.

Newsletter. Quarterly. Professional events and opportunities.

Infoblatt. Occasional papers.

Rundbrief. Pub. 8 times a year. Student newsletter.

Meetings

1990: 22–24 Nov., New Orleans, LA

1991: 23–25 Nov., Washington, DC

The association sponsors the Placement Information Center (PIC) for its members.

Each year AATG, in conjunction with Goethe House, awards outstanding teachers of German the Certificate of Merit.

To support the teaching of German, members may borrow films and videocassettes from the Audio Visual Center at nominal charge and purchase audiomotor units, books, short publications, and teacher-tested classroom strategies from the Printed Materials Center. The Kinder lernen Deutsch! program supports the teaching of German to children in the elementary grades.

Student programs include the National Testing Program for high school students; summer study in Germany; the national secondary school honor society Delta Epsilon Phi; the National German Convention; and the awards program, which offers students all-expenses-paid study trips to West Germany.

In-depth workshops and seminars on the latest topics of pedagogical significance are available to all members through the local chapters. For the cost of transatlantic transportation, members can spend three weeks during the summer living with a family in the Rheinland-Pfalz and attending seminars and lectures or participate in an intensive two week seminar in Wieneck, West Germany. The association also coordinates two two-week study-travel seminars, the East German Landeskundeseminar and Perpectiven: Österreich.

AATG is a member of NFMLTA and JNCL, an organizational member of ACTFL and the Internationaler Deutschlehrerverband, and an allied organization of the MLA.

17.   American Association of Teachers of Italian (AATI)
Department of Romance Languages
Wayne State University
Detroit, MI 48202
Founded 1924
1,700 members
Tel. 313 577-3219
Secretary-Treasurer: Louis Kibler
AATI promotes the study of Italian in the United States and Canada.

Periodicals
Italica. Ed. Edward J. Rodini (618 Van Hise Hall, Univ. of Wisconsin, Madison, WI 53706). Quarterly.
AATI Newsletter. Ed. Salvatore Cappelletti. Semiannual.

AATI has also published *A Handbook for Teachers of Italian,* edited by Anthony S. Mollica (1976).

The association meets annually in conjunction with the American Council on the Teaching of Foreign Languages (see ACTFL).

Competition and awards
AATI High School Language Contest
AATI Outstanding College Essay Contest
AATI Outstanding Achievement Award, presented to a faculty member
Summer Travel Grant to the Universitá per Stranieri di Perugia, awarded to a high school teacher from New York State.

The association runs Corsi di Aggiornamento at the Scuola di Lingua e Cultura Italiana per Stranieri in Siena, under sponsorship of the Italian Ministry of Public Education.

AATI is a member of NFMLTA and is an allied organization of the MLA.

18.   American Association of Teachers of Slavic and East European Languages (AATSEEL)
Foreign Language Department
Arizona State University
Tempe, AZ 85287-0202
Founded 1941
1,700 members
Tel. 602 965-6394
Executive Secretary: Sanford Couch
AATSEEL seeks to advance the study and to promote the teaching of Slavic and East European languages, literatures, and cultures on all levels.

Periodicals
Slavic and East European Journal. Ed. Ernest A. Scatton (Slavic Dept., State Univ. of New York, Albany, NY 12222). Quarterly.
AATSEEL Newsletter.

AATSEEL holds an annual meeting in conjunction with the MLA convention.

19. **American Association of Teachers of Spanish and Portuguese (AATSP)**
Lee Hall 218
Mississippi State University
PO Box 6349
Mississippi State, MS 39762-6349
Founded 1917
12,000 members
Tel. 601 325-2041
Executive Director: James R. Chatham
AATSP encourages the study of Spanish and Portuguese languages and literatures throughout the United States and Canada by the promotion of friendly relations among its members, by the publication of articles, and by the presentation and discussion of papers at the annual meetings. AATSP has seventy-four local chapters.

Periodicals
Hispania. Ed. Theodore Sackett (Dept. of Spanish and Portuguese, Univ. of Southern California, Los Angeles, CA 90089-0358). Quarterly.
Enlace. Pub. 3 times a year. Newsletter.

Meeting: 1990: 10–14 Aug., Miami Beach, FL

The association sponsors the Placement Bureau for its members.

Educational programs include the Sociedad Honoraria Hispánica and the National Spanish Examination for secondary school students; the Oficina Nacional de Correspondencia Escolar, a pen-pal service for Spanish-speaking students; Culture Displays, a series of traveling exhibits; and Bronze and Silver Medals and Certificates of the Association, awarded to outstanding students of Spanish by any member in good standing. The association also consults on pedagogical matters.

AATSP is a member of NFMLTA.

20. **American Association of University Professors (AAUP)**
1012 14th Street, NW
Suite 500
Washington, DC 20005
Founded 1915
42,000 members
Tel. 202 737-5900
Director of Membership and Public Information: Iris Molotsky
AAUP is the only national organization exclusively representing the interests of college and university faculty members across disciplines. AAUP establishes and maintains standards for academic due process and advocates faculty participation in academic governance. The association is best known for its assistance to faculty members whose academic freedom has been violated. Each year AAUP responds to numerous inquiries from faculty members and administrators and reviews more than one thousand formal complaints. AAUP participates in state and federal court cases involving significant academic freedom and tenure issues and maintains a government relations program to monitor legislative appropria-

tions and to provide information and testimony on pending legislation. The association independently gathers salary and compensation data for publication in its annual salary survey, *The Annual Report on the Economic Status of the Profession*. The report, which contains comparisons by institution, rank, and gender, is a valuable resource for faculty members and administrators who rely on its data to determine budgets and salaries.

Active AAUP membership is open to teaching faculty members, professional librarians, and counselors with faculty status at accredited institutions. Additional categories for participation in AAUP include graduate student and public membership.

Periodical: *Academe: Bulletin of the AAUP.* Ed. Paul Strohm. Pub. 6 times a year. General-interest articles related to higher education.

AAUP also publishes collections of major policy statements and reports such as *AAUP Policy Documents and Report* (1984) and *Higher Education Salary Evaluation Kit: A Recommended Method for Flagging Women and Minority Persons for Whom There Is Apparent Salary Inequity and a Comparison of Results and Costs of Several Suggested Methods* (1977).

AAUP convenes each June.

AAUP advances its programs through standing committees including Committee A on Academic Freedom and Tenure, Committee B on Professional Ethics, Committee L on Historically Black Institutions and the Status of Minorities in the Profession, Committee R on Government Relations, and Committee W on the Status of Women in the Academic Profession. Special projects include faculty development and pension plans, the role of faculty in the assessment movement, professional ethics and conflicts of interest in scientific research, increased appointments of part-time and non-tenure-track faculty members.

21.   American Association of University Women (AAUW)
2401 Virginia Avenue
Washington, DC 20037
Founded 1881
140,000 members
Tel. 202 785-7700
Executive Director: Anne Bryant
AAUW promotes equity for women, education and self-development over the life span, and positive societal change. AAUW is the oldest and largest national organization for equity and education.

Periodical: *AAUW Outlook.* Ed. Karen Johnson. Bimonthly.

Publications
College Admissions Tests: Opportunities or Roadblocks?
Coping with Teen Pregnancy: Community Strategies.
Family Leave: A Solution to Work and Family Conflicts.
Progress for Women in Student Financial Aid.

The association meets every two years. The 1991 meeting will be held in Portland, OR.

The AAUW Educational Foundation provides funds nationally and internationally for educational and research fellowships, project grants, and special programs for women. The Legal Advocacy Fund offers funding and a support system for women seeking judicial redress for sex discrimination.

Current programs of AAUW are Promoting Individual Liberties, which calls on individual members to play an activist role in reaffirming constitutional rights and personal opportunities and will build on AAUW action to combat censorship, and Choices for Tomorrow's Women, which recognizes a range of American women's concerns, from pay equity and the roles and value of homemakers and volunteers to career and life-style choices for girls and skill development for women. AAUW's legislative agenda includes the National Child Care Initiative, economic equity, equity in education, family and medical leave, funding for human services, freedom of choice, peace initiatives, and the protection of individual liberties.

AAUW's library and archival collection are available for research by appointment.

22. American Classical League (ACL)
Miami University
Oxford, OH 45056
Founded 1918
3,600 members
Tel. 513 529-4116
Administrative Secretary: Geri Dutra
ACL aims to initiate, improve, and extend the study of classical languages and civilizations; to supplement and reinforce the activities of other classical organizations; and to advance and articulate the cause of liberal education. Members include teachers of Latin, Greek, and classical studies from elementary schools and universities, as well as friends of the classics.

Periodicals
The Classical Outlook. Quarterly.
PRIMA. Semiannual.
ACL Newsletter. Semiannual.

ACL maintains a Teaching Materials and Resource Center that publishes and provides hundreds of teaching aids for teachers at all levels.

The association offers a placement service for teachers of Latin and Greek.

ACL sponsors a National Junior Classical League to promote unity among the thousands of high school Latin students and a National Senior Classical League for those in college.

The association conducts an annual institute to promote excellence in teaching. The 1990 institute will be held at California State University, Northridge.

23. American Comparative Literature Association (ACLA)
Program in Comparative Literature
411 Mason Hall
University of Michigan
Ann Arbor, MI 48109-1027
Founded 1960
700 members
Tel. 313 763-2351
Secretary-Treasurer: Stuart Y. McDougal
ACLA supports and encourages the growth of comparative literature as a discipline in American colleges and universities and seeks to foster an interest in literature as an artistic expression beyond national and linguistic boundaries. Various committees, ad hoc and permanent, report on topics such as criteria for graduate and undergraduate programs in comparative literature, the role of translation in comparative literature, and the relations of literature and the other arts.

Periodicals
Comparative Literature. Ed. Thomas R. Hart and Steven F. Rendall (223 Friendly
    Hall, Univ. of Oregon, Eugene, OR 97403-12333). Quarterly.
ACLA Newsletter. Ed. Stuart Y. McDougal. Semiannual.

Meeting: 1990: 29–31 Mar., Pennsylvania State Univ., University Park, PA; Literature in Global Perspective

ACLA awards two prizes in alternate years for outstanding books in the field of comparative literature: the Harry Levin Prize, for a work of literary history, and the René Wellek Prize, for a work of literary theory.

ACLA is affiliated with the International Comparative Literature Association and is a constituent member of ACLS. Joint memberships are also available with the Canadian Comparative Literature Association and the Southern Comparative Literature Association.

24. American Conference for Irish Studies (ACIS)
Department of English
Marquette University
Milwaukee, WI 53233
Founded 1962
2,000 members
Tel. 414 224-7179
Secretary: Michael Gillespie
The conference seeks to establish a means of communication among scholars in Irish studies in all disciplines and to develop teaching and scholarly inquiry in Irish studies.

Periodicals
Irish Literary Supplement. Ed. Robert Lowery. Semiannual.
ACIS Newsletter. Ed. Robert Lowery. Pub. 3 times a year.

Publication: *A Guide to Irish Studies in the US.* 3rd ed.

ACIS meets each spring and holds regional conferences each fall in the New England, middle Atlantic, midwest, and western states. ACIS also sponsors joint sessions with the American Historical Association, the MLA, and the American Anthropological Association.

25. American Council of Teachers of Russian/American Council for Collaboration in Education and Language Study (ACTR/ACCELS)
1619 Massachusetts Avenue, NW
5th Floor
Washington, DC 20036
Founded 1974
1,500 members
Tel. 202 328-2287; FAX 202 328-8068
Director: Dan Davidson
ACTR is a national educational association and academic exchange organization specializing in Russian language training and field development. ACTR seeks to further the study of Russian in America through a range of training and research exchange programs with the Soviet Union. The ACTR program, begun in the academic year 1975–76, continues to provide Americans the opportunity to study at the foremost center in the Soviet Union for research and study in Russian as a foreign language.

ACCELS was founded in 1987 as a sister organization to ACTR. Not a membership organization, ACCELS administers annual exchanges involving Soviet, Czech, Slovak, and Hungarian students and teachers of English, and American students of Czech, Slovak, and Hungarian. Other ACCELS activities focus on curricular and professional development in the languages of Eastern Europe and the non-Russian languages of the Soviet Union.

Periodical: *ACTR/ACCELS Newsletter.* Pub. 5 times a year.

Publications
Russian: Stage One. Ed. G. Bixextina, D. Davidson, and T. Dorofeeva. Moscow: Russian Language Pubs., 1985.
Russian: Stage Two. Ed. N. Baranova, R. Brecht, D. Davidson, and N. Kostromina. Moscow: Russian Language Pubs., 1985.

ACTR sponsored the International Association of Teachers of Russian Language and Literature (MAPRIAL) Conference, a Soviet-American conference on teaching Russian to nonnative speakers, held 15–20 February 1989 in Washington, DC.

ACTR selects and supports well-qualified high school students through a network of local and regional contests to represent the United States at the International Olympiada for Russian Language held in Moscow every three years.

ACTR/ACCELS administers fellowships for participants in the associations' exchange programs from private and federal grants.

Through direct cooperative agreements with seven Soviet institutes, ACTR sponsors summer, semester, ten-month, and variable-term programs in Moscow and Leningrad for Americans to study advanced Russian and to conduct doctoral and postdoctoral research.

ACTR/ACCELS sponsors an exchange of Russian language teaching professionals from the Soviet Union and English language teachers from the United States. Soviet professors are placed in American universities, colleges, and high schools to provide expertise and to assist in curriculum development. American teachers of English fulfill similar functions at pedagogical institutes in the Soviet Union.

ACCELS sponsors the United States-Hungarian and United States-Czechoslovakian Summer Language Study Exchanges. Each summer a group of approximately thirty students and teachers from Hungary and Czechoslovakia travels to the United States for advanced language training, and a group of American students travel to Hungary and Czechoslovakia for intermediate and advanced training in Hungarian, Czech, or Slovak.

The ACTR/ACCELS research program works to improve the quality of Russian language training in the United States by establishing collaborative textbook projects with Soviet pedagogical specialists and by organizing conferences on the analysis and teaching of Russian. ACTR/ACCELS also supports scholarly research on second-language acquisition, using a computerized database of records from over one thousand Russian language students.

ACTR is part of a three-member consortium selected by the United States government to administer the United States/Soviet Union High School Academic Partnership Program. This program will establish partnerships between American and Soviet high schools over the next three years and will involve approximately fifteen hundred students.

26.   American Council on the Teaching of Foreign Languages (ACTFL)
6 Executive Plaza
Yonkers, NY 10701
Founded 1966
10,000 members
Tel. 914 963-8830
Executive Director: C. Edward Scebold

The mission of ACTFL is to promote and foster the study of languages and cultures as an integral component of American education and society and to provide effective leadership for the improvement of teaching and learning at all levels of instruction. Five current areas are central to ACTFL's mission: curriculum and materials development, proficiency testing, public awareness, research, and teacher education. ACTFL programs and projects range from those influencing instructional policies at the national level to those furnishing practical assistance to classroom teachers.

Periodicals

Foreign Language Annals. Ed. Vicki Galloway. Pub. 6 times a year. Articles on successful teaching methods, educational research or experimentation, and concerns and problems of the profession.
ACTFL Newsletter. Ed. Mary Allison. Quarterly.

One volume of the series Foreign Language Education, edited by Diane Birckbichler (Ohio State Univ.), is published annually. The Materials Center offers foreign language teaching aids, both general and language-specific, and materials on foreign language careers to members at a discount.

ACTFL sponsors workshops the during three days following the annual convention.
    1990: 19-24 Nov., New Orleans, LA; Acting on Priorities
    1991: 23-25 Nov., Washington, DC

The Distinguished Service Awards, administered annually to honor outstanding contributors to foreign language education, recognize published works, achievements in teaching or services, contributions to the teaching of culture in the foreign language classroom, and the promotion of community interest in foreign language education.

Special institutes, seminars, and workshops on familiarization, testing, and curriculum are offered periodically through the ACTFL Professional Development Program.

The Alert Network is an information chain to promote participation in and influence on professional developments in legislation, public policy, and education. ACTFL also supports the Washington liaison office of the Joint National Committee for Languages (JNCL) with other foreign language organizations.

ACTFL offers group insurance plans to members.

27. American Culture Association (ACA)
    Bowling Green State University
    Bowling Green, OH 43403
Founded 1978
1,000 members
Tel. 419 372-2981
Secretary-Treasurer: Ray B. Browne
ACA aims to study the culture of the Americas, especially that of the United States, the influences on it, and its influence on other cultures.

Periodical: *Journal of American Culture.* Ed. Ray B. Browne. Quarterly.

Meetings
    1990: 8-10 Mar., Toronto, ON
    1991: Apr., San Antonio, TX
    1992: Apr., Louisville, KY

28. American Dialect Society (ADS)
    Department of English
    MacMurray College
    Jacksonville, IL 62650
Founded 1889
600 members
Tel. 217 479-7049/7000
Executive Secretary: Allan Metcalf
ADS studies the English language in North America, together with other languages influencing or influenced by it. Standing research committees report on new words, proverbial sayings, regionalisms and linguistic geography, non-English dialects, and usage.

Periodicals

American Speech: A Quarterly of Linguistic Usage. Ed. Ronald R. Butters (English Dept., Duke Univ., Durham, NC 27706).

Newsletter of the American Dialect Society (NADS). Ed. Allan Metcalf. Pub. 3 times a year.

Publication of the American Dialect Society (PADS). Ed. Dennis E. Baron (Dept. of English, Univ. of Illinois, Urbana, IL 61801). Occasional monograph series.

Since its inception, the society's major project has been the preparation of a dialect dictionary for the United States, recently coming to fruition in the *Dictionary of American Regional English* (Harvard UP).

As an affiliated organization of the MLA, ADS sponsors sessions at the MLA convention. ADS is a constituent member of ACLS.

29.   American Economic Association (AEA)
1313 21st Avenue South, Suite 809
Nashville, TN 37212-2786
Founded 1923
26,000 members
Tel. 615 322-2595
President: Joseph A. Pechman

The purposes of the association are the encouragement of economic research, especially the historical and statistical study of the conditions of historical life; the issue of publications on economic subjects; and the promotion of freedom of economic discussion. The association takes no partisan attitude, nor will it commit its members to any position on practical economic questions. Although the majority of members are associated with academic institutions, over a third come from the business and industrial communities.

Periodicals

American Economic Review (AER). Pub. 5 times a year. Articles and short papers on economic subjects; May's issue contains the proceedings of the previous year's annual meeting.

Journal of Economic Literature (JEL). Quarterly. Survey and review articles, abstracts of articles from foreign and domestic economics periodicals, a list of new books, and book reviews. (Online access available through DIALOG Information Retrieval Services.)

Journal of Economic Perspectives (JEP). Quarterly. Accessible articles on recent research and public policy initiatives and insightful readings for classroom use.

Index of Economic Articles. Annual. (Online access available through DIALOG.)

Meeting: 1990: 27–30 Dec., Washington, DC

The National Registry for Economists is a national clearinghouse for economists seeking employment. The bimonthly *Job Openings for Economists* is available by subscription to AEA members. A professional placement service operates at the annual convention.

Contributions to the profession are made by the continuing work of AEA's Committee on Economic Education, Committee on the Status of Minority Groups in the Economics Profession, Committee on the Status of Women in the Economics Profession, and Committee on Political Discrimination.

AEA is a constituent member of ACLS.

30.   American Folklore Society (AFS)
1703 New Hampshire Avenue, NW
Washington, DC 20009
Founded 1888
1,400 members
Tel. 202 232-8800
Executive Secretary-Treasurer: Timothy C. Lloyd
AFS aims to promote, advance, stimulate, and encourage interest and research in, and study of, folklore in all its aspects; to aid in the distribution of the results of such research by publishing reports and journals; and to serve as a bond among those interested in the study of folklore. Members include teachers; professional staff members in museums and in humanities, arts, and educational programs and government agencies; students; and interested individuals.

Periodicals
Journal of American Folklore. Ed. Bruce Jackson (Samuel Clemens Hall, State Univ. of New York, Buffalo, NY 14260). Quarterly.
American Folklore Society Newsletter. Ed. Timothy Lloyd. Bimonthly.

Publication: *Folklore/Folklife.* 1984.

Meetings
1990: 17–21 Oct., Oakland, CA
1991: Oct., St. John's, NF

AFS annually sponsors the Folklore Fellows Prize for the best student work, the Richard Reuss Prize for the best student work on the history of folklore study, the W. W. Newell Prize for the best work on children's folklore, and the Elli Kongas Mirand Prize for the best work on women's folklore. AFS awards one summer-long internship for a graduate student in folklore at a public institution (arts council, historical agency, museum) with a folklore, folklife, or folk arts program.

Although it has no ongoing program, AFS supports occasional lobbying and information efforts on issues of interest and concern to the field.

AFS is a constituent member of ACLS and NHA.

31.   American Historical Association (AHA)
400 A Street, SE
Washington, DC 20003
Founded 1884
13,000 members
Tel. 202 544-2422
Executive Director: Samuel R. Gammon
According to its constitution and bylaws, the purpose of AHA is "the promotion of historical studies through the encouragement of research, teaching, and publication; the collection and preservation of historical documents and artifacts; the

dissemination of historical records and information; the broadening of historical knowledge among the general public; and the pursuit of kindred activities in the interest of history." The members include college and university faculty members, who make up the majority, as well as public historians, independent scholars, librarians and archivists, and secondary school teachers.

Periodicals

American Historical Review. Ed. David Ransel. Pub. 5 times a year.

Perspectives. Ed. Cecilia Dadian. Pub. 9 times a year. Includes employment information.

Recently Published Articles. Ed. Kathy Koziara-Herbert. Pub. 3 times a year. Bibliography.

Doctoral Dissertations in History. Annual.

Grants, Fellowships and Prizes of Interest to Historians. Annual.

Guide to Departments of History. Annual.

Pamphlets

Bicentennial Essays on the Constitution. Forthcoming.

Constitutional Dissenters and Varieties of Constitutionalism. By George M. Dennison.

Federalism in American Constitutional Development. By Harry N. Scheiber.

Learning Liberty: American Constitutional Beginnings to 1803. By John Murrin.

The Presidency and Public Policy. By John A. Rohr.

Studying History: An Introduction to Methods and Structure. Rev. ed. By Paul L. Ward. 1985

Teaching History with Film and Television. By John E. O'Connor. 1987.

The Columbian Voyages, the Columbian Exchange, and Their Historians. By Alfred W. Crosby. 1987.

More than twenty specialized historical groups meet jointly with AHA at its annual meeting.

1990: 27–30 Dec., New York, NY

1991: 27–30 Dec., Chicago, IL

AHA periodically holds regional conferences, conferences on special topics (e.g., on access to Hispanic archive materials), and institutes (e.g., on teaching history with film). The Pacific Coast Branch holds separate meetings and publishes the *Pacific Coast Review.*

AHA members are eligible for research grants: the Albert J. Beveridge Grants for research in the Western Hemisphere; the Michael Kraus Research Grant for research in American colonial history; the Littleton-Griswold Research Grants for research in American legal history and the field of law and society; and the Bernadotte E. Schmitt Grants for research in the history of Europe, Africa, and Asia. AHA also awards twenty prizes for works published in a variety of historical fields.

Sponsored jointly by the Library of Congress and the AHA, the J. Franklin Jameson Fellowship supports significant scholarly research in the Library of Congress by young historians. The National Aeronautics and Space Administration supports the annual NASA Fellowship, which provides applicants of unusual ability significant and sustained research opportunities in NASA aerospace science, technology, management, or policy.

AHA is one of four sponsors of the National Commission on Social Studies in Schools.

Legislative efforts are conducted through the National Coordinating Committee for the Promotion of History, NHA, and the Consortium of Social Science Associations. AHA is a constituent member of the ACLS and is represented on the Social Science Research Council. Over eighty organizations are affiliated with AHA. In its effort to vigorously promote international liaisons with historical groups throughout the world, AHA represents the United States on the International Committee of Historical Sciences (Comité Internationale des Sciences Historiques).

32. American Humor Studies Association (AHSA)
Department of English
Southwest Texas State University
San Marcos, TX 78666
Founded 1974
200 members
Editor: John O. Rosenbalm
The association encourages the study and appreciation of American humor in an interdisciplinary context.

Periodical: *Studies in American Humor.* Ed. John O. Rosenbalm (Dept. of English, Southwest Texas State Univ., San Marcos, TX 87666). Quarterly.

As an affiliated society, AHSA meets in conjunction with the MLA, SAMLA, and other groups.

33. American Hungarian Educators' Association (AHEA)
707 Snider Lane
Silver Spring, MD 20904
Founded 1974
200 members
Tel. 301 384-4659
President: Enikö M. Basa
The association is devoted to the dissemination and study of Hungarian culture — history, folklore, literature, language, fine arts, music, and scientific achievements. AHEA actively supports ethnic and bicultural programs to broaden American and Canadian awareness of Hungarian contributions to North American society, as well as to deepen appreciation of Hungarian culture among ethnic Hungarians and others.

The association publishes its newsletter, the *AHEA Educator*, three times a year.

Meetings
1990: May, Montclair State Coll., Upper Montclair, NJ
1991: Indiana Univ., Bloomington, IN
1992: Univ. of Toronto, Toronto, ON

The association will try to find local contacts or hosts for students.

Affiliates and special sections include the American Hungarian Folklore Centrum, the American Hungarian Librarians Association, and the American Association for the Study of Hungarian History.

34. American Jewish Historical Society (AJHS)
2 Thornton Road
Waltham, MA 02154
Founded 1892
3,500 members
Tel. 617 891-8110; FAX 617 899-9208
Director: Bernard Wax

AJHS is dedicated to the collection, preservation, and distribution of information on the history of Jews on the American continent.

Periodicals

American Jewish History. Ed. Mare Lee Raphael and Jeffrey Gurock. Quarterly. Provides a forum for historical topics such as Jewish Impact on Mass American Culture, American Zionism, Anti-Semitism in America, and America and the Holocaust.
Heritage. Ed. Bernard Wax. Semiannual newsletter.

The society has published the following titles in collaboration with the Institute of Contemporary Jewry, Hebrew University of Jerusalem:
  Guide to America-Holy Land Studies, 1620–1948. Vols. 1–3. Ed. Nathan M. Kaganoff. 1977, 1982, 1983.
  Guide to America-Holy Land Studies, 1620–1948. Vol. 4. Ed. Menahem Kaufman and Mira Levine. 1984.
  With Eyes Toward Zion: Scholars Colloquium on America-Holy Land Studies. 2 vols. Ed. Moshe Davis. 1977, 1986.
  American Jews: The Building of a Voluntary Community. By Eli Ginzburg. Texts and Studies. 1980.
  American Judaism: A Pluralistic Religious Community. By Abraham J. Karp. Texts and Studies. 1984.

AJHS also produces catalogs of its own collections periodically.

An annual national conference covers various themes relating to American Jewish history.
  1990: 18–21 May, Omaha, NE
  1991: May, Hartford, CT
  1992: May, Washington, DC

The society offers awards for articles on local history and student essays and sponsors a National History Day Award for high school students.

AJHS provides speakers and programs for communities and groups throughout the country, as well as reference services to libraries, scholars, students, agencies, and the general public. The society's library contains eighty thousand books and seven million manuscripts, newspapers, and pamphlets documenting the heritage of the American Jewish community; and an extensive Yiddish film collection. The museum in Waltham displays paintings, photographs, documents, and artifacts; mounts special exhibitions such as Jewish Life in America: Fulfilling the American Dream; and assists other exhibiting facilities by supplying materials.

35.   American Literary Translators Association (ALTA)
Box 830688
University of Texas at Dallas
Richardson, TX 75083-0688
Founded 1978
1,000 members
Tel. 214 690-2093
Executive Secretary: Sheryl St. Germain
ALTA aims to enhance the quality of literary translation in the United States and to assist translators.

Periodicals
Translation Review. Ed. Rainer Schulte and Dennis Kratz. Pub. 3 times a year.
ALTA Newsletter. Ed. Elizabeth Miller. Quarterly.

The association holds an annual meeting.

Prizes awarded
Gregory Rabassa Prize for the translation of prose
Richard Wilbur Prize for the translation of poetry
Small-Press Translation Project, grants for translating into any language quality English language fiction published by a small United States press.

36.   American Musicological Society (AMS)
201 South 34th Street
Philadelphia, PA 19104-6313
Founded 1934
3,600 members
Tel. 215 898-8698
Executive Director and Treasurer: Alvin H. Johnson
The society aims to advance research in the fields of music as a branch of learning and scholarship.

AMS publishes the *Journal of the American Musicological Society* three times a year, its newsletter twice a year, and an annual *Directory. Doctoral Dissertations in Musicology*, a list of dissertations in progress and completed at institutions worldwide, published its seventh compilation in 1984. A new series of cumulative editions beginning with 1983 will be published at five-year intervals; the first edition became available in 1989. Annual interim lists provide members with current data.

At the annual meeting members read scholarly papers; participate in study sessions, panel discussions, and forums; and attend concerts and exhibits.
        1990: 8–11 Nov., Oakland, CA; joint meeting with the Society for Music
            Theory and the Society for Ethnomusicology.
        1991: 7–10 Nov., Chicago, IL
        1992: 5–8 Nov., Pittsburgh, PA

AMS's fifteen chapters (covering all of the USA and Canada) hold meetings and bring the activity of the society to a local level.

Prizes awarded
Einstein Award for the best article by a young scholar
Kinkeldey Award for the best book
Greenberg Award for support of a performance-orientated project

In 1989, the society completed a four-year campaign to raise five million dollars in capital funds to endow one-year fellowships awarded to doctoral candidates in the dissertation-writing year of their education.

AMS cooperates with the International Musicological Society, the Music Library Association, the Society for Music Theory, the Society for Ethnomusicology, the Sonneck Society, and the College Music Society in undertakings of common interest. AMS is a constituent member of ACLS.

37.   American Name Society (ANS)
Department of Romance Languages
Baruch College
17 Lexington Avenue
New York, NY 10010
Founded 1951
1,100 members
Tel. 212 505-2177
Executive Secretary-Treasurer: Wayne H. Finke
The society studies the etymology, origin, meaning, and application of all categories of names — geographical, personal, scientific, commercial and popular — and distributes the findings. Members include professors of language and literature, psychology, and sociology; cartographers; and students of onomastics.

Periodicals
Names. Ed. Thomas Gasque (English Dept., Univ. of South Dakota, Vermillion, SD 57069). Quarterly.
ANS Bulletin.

ANS convenes annually in November; the society also sponsors sessions at the MLA convention, and members participate in national onomastic symposia and conferences.

38.   American Philological Association (APA)
Department of Classics
Fordham University
Bronx, NY 10458-5154
Founded 1869
3,000 members
Tel. 212 579-2994
Secretary-Treasurer: Harry B. Evans
APA is the principal learned society in North America in the field of classical studies, with membership comprising mainly college and university teachers of

classical languages, literature, and history. Its purpose is the advancement and diffusion of philological knowledge.

Periodicals
Transactions of the American Philological Association. Ed. Ruth Scodel (Univ. of Michigan). Annual.
APA Newsletter. Ed. Harry B. Evans. Bimonthly.

APA maintains a publishing program carried out by the Scholars Press, a consortium of learned societies and educational institutions that has pioneered low-cost means of disseminating scholarly work. Two monograph series, the Philological Monographs and American Classical Studies, provide publication activities for various types of book-length manuscripts. The Textbook Series publishes texts of classical authors at all levels of language and literature courses. A microfiche program administered through Classical Micropublishing, Inc., jointly sponsored with the American Society of Papyrologists, makes research materials widely and cheaply available on film.

The annual meeting is held jointly with the Archaeological Institute of America (see AIA). The program includes an APA-AIA Joint Session, panels, seminars, and meetings of affiliated groups like the Vergilian Society and the American Classical League.
> 1990: 27–30 Dec., San Francisco, CA
> 1991: 27–30 Dec., Chicago, IL
> 1992: 27–30 Dec., New Orleans, LA

APA operates a placement service for AIA and itself and issues *Positions for Classicists and Archaeologists* monthly.

The Charles J. Goodwin Award of Merit recognizes outstanding scholarship in classical studies, and the Awards for Excellence in the teaching of classics honor outstanding teachers of undergraduate classical studies. APA awards a fellowship for work at the *Thesaurus Linguae Latinae* in Munich each year.

The Campus Advisory Service assists colleges and universities in initiating or developing humanities programs with classical orientations, in reviewing or revising existing programs, and in developing new approaches. Active committees of the association include the Committee on Computer Activities, the Committee on the Classical Tradition in North America, the Committee on the Status of Women and Minority Groups, and the Committee on Regional Associations.

APA is a member of the National Committee on Latin and Greek and of NHA. The association is affiliated with the Fédération International des Associations d'Etudes Classiques (FIEC) and is a constituent society of ACLS.

39.   American Philosophical Association (APA)
       University of Delaware
       Newark, DE 19716
Founded 1900
8,000 members
Tel. 302 451-1112
Executive Director: David A. Hoekema

APA promotes the exchange of ideas among philosophers, encourages creative and scholarly work in philosophy, and facilitates the professional work of teachers of philosophy.

Proceedings and Addresses of the American Philosophical Association, including presidential addresses, convention programs, and meeting reports, appears seven times each academic year. APA also issues *Jobs for Philosophers* five times a year and newsletters in two or three combined issues each year on philosophy and medicine, philosophy and feminism, philosophy and law, computer use, and teaching philosophy.

Other APA publications include *The Guidebook for Publishing Philosophy*, a *Guidebook to Graduate Study in Philosophy*, *Philosophy: A Brief Guide for Undergraduates*, and *Careers for Philosophers*.

Three meetings are held each year, one on the East Coast in late December, one in the Midwest in late April, and one on the Pacific Coast in March.
    1990: 28–31 Mar., Los Angeles, CA; Pacific Div.
           25–28 Apr., New Orleans, LA; Central Div.
           27–30 Dec., Boston, MA; Eastern Div.
    1991: Mar., San Francisco, CA; Pacific Div.
           Apr., Chicago, IL; Central Div.
           27–30 Dec., New York, NY; Eastern Div.

Prizes and honors awarded
Matchette Prize for the best book by a younger philosopher
Carus Lectureship for a distinguished professor
Patrick Romanell Lectureship in Philosophical Naturalism
Josiah Royce Lectureship in the Philosophy of Mind
Alfred Schutz Lectureship
David Baumgardt Memorial Lectureship

APA is affiliated with the International Federation of Societies of Philosophy and is a constituent member of ACLS.

40. American Political Science Association (APSA)
    1527 New Hampshire Avenue, NW
    Washington, DC 20036
Founded 1903
13,700 members
Tel. 202 483-2512
Executive Director: Catherine Rudder
APSA is the major professional organization in the United States for persons engaged in the study of politics. The association provides members with services to facilitate research, teaching, and professional development.

Periodicals
The American Political Science Review. Ed. Sammuel C. Patterson. Quarterly.
PS: Political Science and Politics. Ed. Robert J.P. Hauck. Quarterly.
The Political Science Teacher. Ed. Sheilah Mabb. Quarterly.

APSA publishes professional and instructional materials. Works for the classroom include *Congress: We the People*, a telecourse; *Setups: American Politics*, computer-related instructional materials; and monographs on women and government and on other political issues.

Meetings
>1990: 30 Aug.–2 Sept., San Francisco, CA
>1991: 29 Aug.–1 Sept., Washington, DC
>1992: 3–6 Sept., Chicago, IL

The association sponsors the monthly *Personnel Service Newsletter*, a placement service at the annual meeting, and several publications on careers.

APSA awards nineteen prizes, ranging from dissertation, book, and paper awards to recognition of lifetime achievement. The Congressional Fellowships allow academics and journalists to work for nine months on the staffs of members of Congress. APSA also sponsors Black American Fellowships and Chicano-Latino Fellowships. APSA holds an annual Summer Institute for Black Undergraduates.

APSA is a constituent member of ACLS.

41. American Society for Aesthetics (ASA)
4-108 Humanities Centre
University of Alberta
Edmonton, AB T6G 2E5, Canada
Founded 1942
890 members
Tel. 403 492-4102
Secretary-Treasurer: Roger A. Shiner
The purpose of the society is to promote study, research, discussion, and publication in aesthetics. The term aesthetics includes all studies of the arts and related types of experience from a philosophic, scientific, or other theoretical standpoint, including those of psychology, sociology, anthropology, cultural history, art criticism, and education. The arts include the visual arts, literature, music, and theater.

Periodicals
Journal of Aesthetics and Art Criticism. Ed. Donald W. Crawford. Quarterly.
ASA Newsletter. Pub. 3 times a year.

Meetings include an annual convention and meetings held by the three regional divisions: Eastern, Rocky Mountain, and Pacific.
>1990: 25–28 Oct., Austin, TX

The society plans to sponsor a summer institute on the philosophy and history of the arts in 1991.

ASA is a constituent member of the ACLS.

42.   American Society for Eighteenth-Century Studies (ASECS)
University of Cincinnati — M. L. 368
721 Old Chemistry Building
Cincinnati, OH 45221-0368
Founded 1969
1,970 members
Tel. 513 556-3820
Executive Secretary: Edward P. Harris
The aim of the society is to advance study and research in the history of eighteenth-century culture. ASECS works through its publications and meetings to foster interest and encourage investigation, among students of all branches of learning, in the achievements of that century. Membership is open to all persons interested in the society's purposes, including academicians, graduate students, museum and library staff members, and scholars and others with no formal institutional ties.

Periodicals
Eighteenth-Century Studies. Ed. Robert Hopkins and Arthur McGuinness (Dept. of English, Univ. of California, Davis, CA 95616). Quarterly.
Studies in Eighteenth-Century Culture. Ed. Leslie Ellen Brown and Patricia Craddock. Annual. Outstanding papers from the annual meeting.
ASECS News Circular. Ed. Edward P. Harris. Quarterly.

Publication: *Teaching the Eighteenth-Century: Three Courses.* By Cynthia L. Caywood, Nelson Hilton, and Lance E. Wilcox. 1989.

Meetings
    1990: 24–29 Apr., Minneapolis, MN
    1991: 10–14 Apr., Pittsburgh, PA
    1992: Spring, Seattle, WA
Affiliated societies host meetings at various sites throughout the year.

Prizes awarded
James L. Clifford Prize for the best article in the field of eighteenth-century studies
Louis Gottschalk Prize for the book judged to be the most distinguished scholarly contribution to the field of eighteenth-century studies
Graduate Student Paper Prize for a paper presented at the annual meeting

ASECS sponsors a teaching competition each year. The society awards fellowships in conjunction with the American Antiquarian Society, the William Andrews Clark Memorial Library, the Folger Library and Institute, the McMaster University Library, the Newberry Library, and the Yale Center for British Art.

The society has been affiliated with the International Society for Eighteenth-Century Studies (ISECS) since 1969. ISECS sponsors the quadrennial International Congresses on the Enlightenment, held in cities such as Brussels (1983) and Budapest (1987). The society has been a constituent member of the ACLS since 1976.

43.   American Society for Ethnohistory (ASE)
The Newberry Library
60 West Walton
Chicago, IL 60610

Founded 1954
1,200 (individual and institutional) members
Tel. 219 875-7237
Secretary-Treasurer: William O. Autry
The aim of the society is to promote the joint use of documentary materials and ethnographic data, as well as of historiographic and anthropological approaches, in the study of social and cultural processes and history.

Periodical: *Ethnohistory.* Ed. Shepard Krech III (George Mason Univ.). Quarterly. Articles, review essays, and book reviews written by scholars in anthropology, history, linguistics, art history, geography, and other disciplines.

Publication: *Readings from Ethnohistory.* Forthcoming.

Meeting: 1990: 1–4 Nov., Toronto, ON

Prizes awarded
Erminie Wheeler-Voeglelin Prize for a book-length presentation
Robert F. Heizer Prize for an article presentation

44. American Society for Theatre Research (ASTR)
     Theatre Arts Program
     University of Pennsylvania
     Philadelphia, PA 19104-6273
Founded 1956
700 members
Tel. 215 898-5271/7382
Secretary: Cary M. Mazer
The purpose of the society is to promote theater scholarship, to increase knowledge of and appreciation for the history of theater, and to serve the scholarly needs of historians of the theater. Members include theater historians, theater librarians and archivists, dramaturgs, and all others interested in the history of theater.

Periodicals
Theatre Survey. Ed. Roger W. Herzl (Dept. of Theatre, Indiana Univ., Bloomington, IN 47405). Semiannual.
ASTR Newsletter. Semiannual.
International Bibliography of Theatre. Annual.

Publications
Index to the Portraits in Odell's Annals of the New York Stage.
Memoir of John Durang.
Innovations in Stage and Theatre Design.
Bernard Shaw's Arms and the Man.
Edward Gordon Craig and the Pretenders.

Meeting: 1990: 15–18 Nov., Toronto, ON

ASTR awards the Young Scholars Prize for the best published essay by an untenured scholar. The ASTR Fellowship funds travel for a graduate student to a national or international meeting.

Plans to sponsor summer institutes in theater history are pending.

ASTR participates in the International Research and Exchanges Board (IREX) with the Soviet Union.

ASTR represents the United States in the International Federation for Theatre Research and is a constituent member of ACLS.

45.   American Society of Geolinguistics (ASG)
        PO Box 6337, FDR Station
        New York, NY 10150
Founded 1965
66 members
Treasurer: B. L. Richardson
The society gathers and disseminates up-to-date knowledge concerning the world's present-day languages: their distribution and population use; their relative practical importance, usefulness, and availability from economic, political, and cultural standpoints; their genetic, historical, and geographic affiliations and relations; and their identification and use in spoken and written form.

ASG publishes the annual *Geolinguistics*, edited by Jesse Levitt (485 Brooklawn Ave., Fairfield, CT 06432).

Members gather four or five times each academic year.

46.   American Society of Indexers (ASI)
        1700 18th Street, NW
        Washington, DC 20009
Founded 1968
800 members
Tel. 718 990-6200
President: Nancy Mulvany
ASI promotes indexing as a profession and provides information, guidance, and aid to indexers. ASI acts as the advisory body on the qualifications and remuneration of indexers, to which authors, editors, publishers, and others may apply for guidance. Indexers and interested librarians, archivists, publishers, information specialists, researchers, and computer programmers working in this area are welcome to join.

Periodicals
ASI Newsletter. Ed. Nancy Mulvany. Pub. 5 times a year.
The Indexer. Ed. Hazel Bell. Semiannual.
The Register of Indexers. Annual biographical directory of ASI members and their
        areas of subject expertise.

Publications
A Guide to Indexing Software. By Linda K. Fetters.
Generic Markup of Electronic Index Manuscripts. By Hugh C. Maddocks. 1988.
Guide to Freelance Indexing. By Cynthia A. Weber. Rev. ed. 1988.

The association meets each spring. The 1990 meeting will be held in Chicago, IL.

ASI awards the H. W. Wilson Company Indexing Prize.

The association sponsors occasional seminars.

47.   American Sociological Association (ASA)
        1722 N Street, NW
        Washington, DC 20036
Founded 1905
12,400 members
Tel. 202 833-3410
Executive Officer: William V. D'Antonio
ASA seeks to stimulate and improve research, instruction, and discussion in the field of sociology and to encourage cooperative relations among persons engaged in the scientific study of society.

ASA publishes nine journals. The following are of interest to teachers of language and literature:

   American Sociological Review. Ed. Gerald Maxwell. Bimonthly. Works of interest to the discipline in general.

   Contemporary Sociology. Ed. Ida Harper Simpson. Bimonthly. Reviews and critical discussions of recent works in sociology and related disciplines.

   Sociological Theory. Ed. Alan Sica. Pub. spring and fall.

   Sociology of Education. Ed. Philip Wexler. Quarterly.

   Teaching Sociology. Ed. Theodore Wagenaar. Quarterly.

ASA prints pamphlets for students and teachers on numerous topics, including employment opportunities, the sociology major, and the treatment of gender in research. ASA also sponsors the publication of the Rose Monograph Series by Cambridge University Press and other titles by commercial presses.

Meetings
        1990: 11–15 Aug., Washington, DC
        1991: 23–27 Aug., Cincinnati, OH

ASA issues the *Employment Bulletin* monthly.

The association awards six major prizes and sponsors the Minority Fellowship Program.

Lobbying efforts are conducted through the Consortium of Social Science Associations (COSSA).

ASA is a constituent member of ACLS.

48.   American Studies Association (ASA)
        2140 Taliaferro Hall
        University of Maryland
        College Park, MD 20742
Founded 1951
3,500 members
Tel. 301 454-2533
Executive Director: John F. Stephens
ASA's members come from many fields: history, art, literature, science, folklore, ethnic studies, anthropology, museum studies, sociology, government, popular culture, gender studies, and others. They approach American culture from many

directions but have in common the desire to view America as a whole rather than from the perspective of a single discipline.

Periodicals

American Quarterly. Ed. Gary Kulik. Quarterly.

ASA Newsletter. Quarterly. Includes lists of meetings, fellowships, grants, and employment opportunities.

Meetings

    1990: 1–5 Nov., New Orleans, LA

    1991: 31 Oct.–3 Nov., Baltimore, MD

Prizes awarded

John Hope Franklin Publication Prize for the best book in American studies

Ralph Henry Gabriel Dissertation Prize for the best completed dissertation specifically in the field

Bode-Pearson Prize for outstanding contribution to American studies

Wise-Susman Prize for the best student paper presented at the annual meeting

Annette K. Baxter Awards, providing travel assistance to outstanding graduate students on the annual meeting program

American Studies Curriculum Resources make available course outlines and bibliographies in a wide variety of areas, ranging from introductory American studies courses to graduate seminars on special topics.

Members belong to one of twelve regional chapters, many of which issue newsletters and all of which meet at least once a year.

ASA is a constituent member of ACLS.

49.   Archaeological Institute of America (AIA)

    675 Commonwealth Avenue

    Boston, MA 02215

Founded 1879

8,000 members

Tel. 617 353-9361

Executive Director: Mark Meister

AIA is dedicated to the encouragement and support of archaeological research and publication and to the protection of the world's cultural heritage. Members of the institute have conducted excavations in Africa, Asia, Europe, and North and South America. AIA has further promoted archaeological studies by founding research centers and schools in seven countries.

Periodicals

Archaeology. Ed. Peter Young. Bimonthly. Written for the public at large.

American Journal of Archaeology. Ed. Fred S. Kleiner. Quarterly. Studies of art and archaeology of ancient Europe and the Mediterranean world from prehistoric to late antique times.

The annual meeting is held jointly with the American Philological Association (see APA). The program includes an APA-AIA Joint Session, panels, seminars, and meetings of affiliated groups like the Vergilian Society and the American Classical League.

1990: 27–30 Dec., San Francisco, CA
1991: 27–30 Dec., Chicago, IL

APA operates a placement service in conjunction with AIA and publishes *Positions for Classicists and Archaeologists* monthly. AIA's annual *Archaeological Fieldwork Opportunities Bulletin* lists international field excavation opportunities for volunteers.

The institute awards two gold medals each year, one for distinguished archaeological achievement and one for scientific contributions to archaeology. AIA awards two annual fellowships for archaeological research: the Olivia James Traveling Fellowship for travel to Greece, the Aegean Islands, Sicily, southern Italy, Asia Minor, or Mesopotamia; and the Harriet Pomerance Fellowship for travel to pursue a scholarly project in Aegean Bronze Age archaeology.

AIA sponsors tours—each led by a prominent scholar—for members to many parts of the world. Itineraries include visits to see art and architecture, archaeological sites, current excavations, and museums. The eighty-six local societies of the institute sponsor lectures, field trips, films, and museum visits. Each year, AIA awards grants to assist two societies in funding locally organized symposia. Part of each grant subsidizes the publication of the proceedings.

AIA is a constituent member of ACLS.

50. **Association des Professeurs de Français des Universités et Collèges du Canada (APFUCC)**
Department of French
University of Victoria
Victoria, BC V8W 242, Canada
Founded 1958
350 members
President: Danielle Thaler
The association provides opportunities for Canadian teachers of French to meet and discuss their work on the language, literatures, and cultures of French-speaking peoples. APFUCC addresses professional and administrative issues of interest to its members, promotes in Canada the study of French and francophone cultures, encourages individual and collective research in these fields, and collaborates with other organizations having parallel goals.

Periodical: *Nouvelles de L'APFUCC.* Ed. Danielle Thaler. Semiannual.

Publications
Dans les trous du discours. By Irène Pagès and Marguerite Duras. 1987.
Littérature pour la jeunesse: La croisée des chemins. By Danielle Thaler. 1988.
Jeanne Hyvard: La langue d'avenir. By Jennifer Waelti-Walters. 1988.

The association holds its annual meeting in May.

APFUCC sponsors annual prizes for the best article and book in French by a member on the language, literature, or culture of France, Canada, or other French-speaking countries.

51.   Association for Asian Studies (AAS)
1 Lane Hall
University of Michigan
Ann Arbor, MI 48109
Founded 1941
6,800 members
Tel. 313 665-2490
President: Stanley J. Tambiah
AAS is a scholarly, nonpolitical, professional association open to all persons interested in Asia and the study of Asia. Through publications, meetings, and seminars the association seeks to facilitate contact and exchange of information among scholars and to increase understanding of Asia.

Periodicals
The Journal of Asian Studies. Quarterly.
Bibliography of Asian Studies. Annual.
Asian Studies Newsletter. Pub. 5 times a year.
Doctoral Dissertations on Asia. Annual.

Several of the association's committees and special-interest groups sponsor newsletters. AAS's monographs, occasional papers and reference series emphasize mature, critical scholarship based on sources in Asian languages.

AAS helps support eight annual regional conferences and holds a 3-day national meeting each spring.
        1990: 6–8 Apr., Chicago, IL
        1991: 12–14 Apr., New Orleans, LA
        1992: 2–5 Apr., Washington, DC

The association provides a placement service at the annual meeting, and the newsletter has a professional personnel registry section.

AAS awards an annual Distinguished Service Award.

The association's four councils—Northeast Asia, China and Inner Asia, Southeast Asia, and South Asia—guarantee each area a proportionate voice on the Board of Directors. Committees focus on a wide variety of interests, ranging from individual countries to general economic, historical, and pedagogical issues.

AAS is a constituent member of ACLS.

52.   Association for Communication Administration (ACA)
311 Wilson Hall
Murray State University
Murray, KY 42071
Founded 1971
700 members
Tel. 502 762-3411
Executive Director: Vernon W. Gantt
ACA serves the needs of departmental administrators in the communication arts and sciences. The association's goals are to advance the interests of the discipline in colleges and universities; to serve as a forum for the discussion of basic issues

relating to communication, radio-television-film, speech, and theater as disciplines in higher education; to facilitate communication among departmental and higher administrative personnel and to provide means for collecting and disseminating important information; to encourage the development of general policies relating to staff members, administration, curriculum, assistantships, fellowships, and other related matters; and to provide a means for making effective, in academic affairs and in matters affecting the public interest, the opinions and aims of the profession.

Articles in the quarterly *ACA Bulletin* cover topics such as artistic accountability, unionization, internship programs, departmental management, ethnic programs, placement studies, grants, administrators and the law, and rating of doctoral programs.

Publications
Careers in Communication Arts and Science.
Communication Media in Higher Education: A Directory of Academic Programs and Faculty in Radio-Television-Film and Related Media. Rev. ed. 1990.
Directory of Theatre Programs. 4th ed. 1990.
Handbook for Theatre Department Chairs. Ed. Jon Whitmore.

Meeting: 1990: 30–31 Oct., Chicago, IL

ACA operates a Clearinghouse on Faculty Exchange to assist administrators in staffing visiting or exchange professorships. ACA sponsors an annual seminar for experienced administrators within and outside the profession to discuss departmental leadership strategies, problem-solving tactics, and on general attitudes for survival in academic administration. The association's Academic Consultant Service provides departments with screened and competent evaluators for on-campus consultation. Areas of specialization range from rhetorical and communication theory, organizational communication, and communication research methodologies to audiology and deaf education, theater arts, and mass communication.

53. Association for Computers and the Humanities (ACH)
Humanities Research Center
Brigham Young University
Provo, UT 84602
Founded 1978
350 members
Tel. 801 378-3511
Executive Secretary: Randall Jones
ACH is an international organization devoted to encouraging the development and use of computing techniques in humanities research and education. Traditionally, ACH has fostered computer-aided research in literature and language, history, philosophy, anthropology, and related social sciences as well as computer use in the creation and study of art, music, and dance. As computing applications in the humanities have developed and broadened in the 1980s, the association has expanded its scope to include areas from word processing to computer-assisted instruction in composition, language, history, philosophy, and anthropology, as well as computational linguistics and cognitive science, which overlap increasingly with the work in humanities computing.

Periodical: *ACH Newsletter.* Ed. Vicky Walsh (2221 Bunche Hall, UCLA, Los Angeles, CA). Quarterly.

The ninth International Conference for Computers and the Humanities was held 5–10 June 1989 at the University of Toronto, ON.

ACH is an allied organization of the MLA.

54.   Association for Hispanic Classical Theater (AHCT)
    Department of Classical and Romance Languages
    Texas Tech University
    Lubbock, TX 79409
President: Donald T. Dietz
The association is dedicated to promoting greater appreciation for Spain's classical drama in production. The primary work of the association is to make and collect videotapes of *comedias, autos sacramentales,* and adaptations of other works from the Spanish Renaissance and baroque and to provide support materials including roundtable discussions of plays, presentations of theater history, and other programs of interest to teachers, directors, scholars, and anyone else interested in the Golden Age theater. A major project of the association is to catalog, copy, and make available the vast documentation of the Chamizal Golden Age Theater Festival archives. Members may borrow any videotape for a modest handling charge.

The association meets annually in early March in El Paso, TX.

55.   Association for the Advancement of Baltic Studies (AABS)
    111 Knob Hill Road
    Hackettstown, NJ 07840
Founded 1968
1,000 members
Tel. 201 852-5258
Executive Director: Janis Gaigulis
AABS promotes research and education in Baltic studies. Its activities include sponsorship of meetings and conferences for the exchange of scholarly views, promotion and evaluation of research in Baltic studies, and distribution of news of current interest in the area of Baltic studies.

Periodicals
Journal of Baltic Studies. Ed. Laurence Kitching (Simon Fraser Univ., Burnaby, BC V5A 1S6, Canada). Quarterly.
AABS Newsletter. Ed. Yana Okolo-Kulaks. Quarterly.

AABS provides publication subsidies for books and monographs on Baltic subjects. Recent titles include
    The Chronicle of Balthasar Russow. Trans. Jerry C. Smith, Juergen Eichhoff, and William L. Urban. Ed. Valdis J. Zeps. Madison: Univ. of Wisconsin Baltic Studies Center, 1988.
    Linguistics and Poetics of Latvian Folk Songs. Ed. Vaira Vikis-Freibergs. Montreal: McGill-Queen's UP, 1988.

The association convenes biannually. The next meeting will be held 20–23 June 1990 at the University of Washington, Seattle, WA. AABS offers fellowships to support graduate student participation.

AABS awards the Vitols Prize for the best article published in the *Journal of Baltic Studies* since the last conference.

56. Association for the Study of Afro-American Life and History (ASALH)
1407 14th Street, NW
Washington, DC 20005
Founded 1915
2,000 members
Tel. 202 667-2822
Executive Director: Karen Robinson

ASALH promotes the study of black history through publications, branches, and annual meetings.

Periodicals
Journal of American History. Ed. Alton Hornston. Quarterly.
Negro History Bulletin. Ed. Karen Robinson. Quarterly.

For information regarding book publications, write the Associated Publishers (1407 14th St., NW, Washington, DC 20006).

Meetings
1990: 24–28 Oct., Chicago, IL
1991: Washington, DC

A vacancy-announcement file is available for all members.

The association sponsors National History Day Awards and Senior and Junior Prizes in black history.

57. Association for the Study of American Indian Literatures (ASAIL)
Department of English
University of Alaska
Fairbanks, AK 99701
300 members
President: James Ruppert

ASAIL fosters the teaching and study of traditional and contemporary American Indian literatures, both oral and written, through seminars, publications, and dissemination of information.

Periodicals
SAIL: Studies in American Indian Literatures. Ed. Helen Jaskoski (Dept. of English, California State Univ., Fullerton, CA 92364). Quarterly.
ASAIL Newsletter. Ed. John Purdy (Central Oregon Community Coll., Bend, OR 97701). Quarterly.

ASAIL meets annually at the MLA convention.

58.   Association for the Study of Dada and Surrealism
425 EPB, University of Iowa
Iowa City, IA 52242
Founded 1970
500 members
Tel. 319 335-0330
President: Albert Sonnenfeld
Vice President and Secretary: Rudolf E. Kuenzli
The association provides a network for researchers in the interdisciplinary field of Dada and surrealism and furthers a wide range of approaches to the verbal and visual products of the two movements, which are seen in their least limited senses as historical and living phenomena.

Periodical: *Dada/Surrealism.* Ed. Mary Ann Caws and Rudolf E. Kuenzli. Annual.

Publications
New York Dada. 1986.
Dada and Surrealist Film. 1987.
Marcel Duchamp: Artist of the Century. 1988.
André Breton Today. 1989.

The association meets twice a year, at the MMLA annual meeting and the MLA convention. Future topics include Dada in Zurich, in 1989; Surrealism and Its Other, in 1990; and, in 1991, Neo-Dada.

The International Dada Archive at the University of Iowa provides documents to researchers in Dada and surrealism.

59.   Association of Canadian University Teachers of English (ACUTE)
Department of English
University of Saskatchewan
Saskatoon, SK S7N 0W0, Canada
Founded 1952
950 members
Tel. 306 966-5517
President: Len Findlay
ACUTE's aim is "to foster the study of the English language, and literature in English, in Canadian universities."

The association's quarterly journal, *English Studies in Canada* (ed. Douglas Wurtelle, Carleton Univ.), publishes articles solicited from members and the Canadian academic community and covers the whole range of English studies. The association also publishes the *ACUTE Newsletter.*

ACUTE's annual conference, held in late May, emphasizes the scholarly work of the membership and their pedagogical concerns.
    1990: May, Univ. of Victoria, Victoria, BC
    1991: May, Queen's Univ., Kingston, ON
    1992: May, Univ. of Prince Edward Island, PE

ACUTE sponsors the Employment Register of the Canadian Association of Chairs of English (CACE), and the association's Standing Committee on Professional Concerns investigates employment-related issues.

ACUTE occasionally sponsors special conferences—such as the National Forum on Underemployment or Unemployment of Graduates in the Humanities, held in November 1988—in conjunction with other Canadian learned societies and under the aegis of the Canadian Federation for the Humanities.

ACUTE participates in the annual Lobby on Parliament Hill organized by the Canadian Federation for the Humanities. At the annual general meeting, members pass occasional motions regarding censorship, civil liberties, and related matters.

60. Association of Departments of English (ADE)
     10 Astor Place
     New York, NY 10003-6981
Founded 1963
850 departments
Tel. 212 614-6317/6318
Director: David Laurence
ADE has been a part of the MLA since 1965 (see MLA). As the professional organization for chairs and other administrators of college and university English departments, ADE provides forums for discussion of issues in the field and in departmental administration, promotes activities that support good practice in postsecondary teaching of English, and serves as a source of information concerning developments in the field.

ADE Bulletin, edited by David Laurence and published three times a year, addresses intellectual, pedagogical, and professional issues in the field of English at the postsecondary level.

ADE cooperates with the MLA in producing books and pamphlets, such as *A Checklist and Guide for Reviewing Departments of English* (1985), to meet professional needs.

The association sponsors sessions at conventions of the MLA, NCTE, and CCCC.

The Francis March Award honors outstanding contributions to the profession of English in postsecondary teaching and scholarship.

ADE holds three regional seminars each summer. In 1990, Seminar East will be held 21–24 June at the Univ. of Pennsylvania, Philadelphia; Seminar Midwest, 31 May–3 June, Indiana Univ., Bloomington; Seminar West, 12–15 July, Univ. of British Columbia, Vancouver.

The ad hoc committee studies and reports on topics in English education at the post-secondary level as charged by the ADE Executive Council.

61. **Association of Departments of Foreign Languages (ADFL)**
     10 Astor Place
     New York, NY 10003-6981
Founded 1969
1,000 departments
Tel. 212 614-6320
Director: Judith Ginsberg
Established in 1969 under the sponsorship of the MLA (see MLA), ADFL provides college and university chairpersons with a forum for discussion and exchange of ideas on professional matters. Working within the MLA, ADFL serves as a channel of communication among departments and as a voice of the language teaching profession. The nine-member Executive Committee is broadly representative of the membership at large, consisting of chairpersons from two-year institutions, BA/MA-granting institutions, and PhD-granting institutions.

ADFL Bulletin, edited by Judith Ginsberg and published three times a year, presents timely reports on innovative and successful foreign language programs at colleges and universities and addresses a wide range of professional, pedagogical, and governance issues.

ADFL cooperates with the MLA in producing books and pamphlets, such as the *Directory of Master's Programs in Foreign Languages, Foreign Literatures, and Linguistics* (1987), to meet professional needs.

ADFL sponsors sessions at the annual conventions of the MLA and ACTFL and has also sponsored meetings at MMLA, SCMLA, and NEMLA. ADFL's regional affiliate, South Atlantic–ADFL, meets during the convention of SAMLA.

Since 1971 ADFL has held summer seminars for administrators of foreign language and literature departments.

62. **Association of Teachers of Japanese (ATJ)**
     Department of East Asian Languages and Literature
     Van Hise Hall
     University of Wisconsin
     Madison, WI 53707
Founded 1961
750 members
Tel. 608 262-0689
President: James O'Brien
ATJ promotes the exchange of ideas, information, and experience relevant to the concerns of its members; encourages the development and dissemination of superior methods of teaching the Japanese language, linguistics, and literature; and facilitates communication, cooperation, and professional friendship among members.

Periodicals
Journal of the American Teachers of Japanese. Semiannual.
ATJ Newsletter. Pub. 3 times a year. Includes notices of positions available.

The annual meeting is held in March or April in conjunction with the Association for Asian Studies (see AAS).

The association is currently developing a Japanese language proficiency test in cooperation with the United States–Japan Friendship Commission and the Educational Testing Service.

ATJ is a member of JNCL/CLOIS.

63. Association of Teachers of Technical Writing (ATTW)
Department of English
Texas Tech University
Lubbock, TX 79409-3091
Founded 1973
1,000 members
Tel. 806 742-2501
Executive Secretary-Treasurer: Carolyn Rude
ATTW encourages dialogue among teachers of technical communication and promotes technical communication as an academic discipline.

Periodical: *The Technical Writing Teacher.* Ed. Victoria M. Mikelonis (Dept. of Rhetoric, Univ. of Minnesota, St. Paul). Pub. 3 times a year. Includes articles on research, theory, and teaching methods as well as reviews of books and software, news items, and approaches to teaching. The Fall issue addresses a special research topic in depth and includes an annual bibliography.

ATTW also publishes anthologies of materials on teaching technical communication, each with a bibliography. Recent titles include *Professional Writing: Toward a College Curriculum*, edited by Barbara Couture, and *The Case Method in Technical Communication*, edited by R. John Brockmann.

ATTW meets annually in conjunction with CCCC (see NCTE) and also sponsors sections at the MLA convention.

64. Bibliographical Society of America (BSA)
PO Box 397
Grand Central Station
New York, NY 10163
Founded 1904
1,500 members
Tel. 718 832-1060
Executive Secretary: Marjory Zaik
Membership in the BSA is open to all those interested in bibliographical problems and projects.

Periodical: *Papers of the Bibliographical Society of America.* Ed. William S. Peterson (Dept. of English, Univ. of Maryland, College Park, MD 20742). Quarterly.

Publications
Tauchnitz International Editions in English, 1841–1955: A Bibliographical History. By William B. Todd and Ann Bowden. 1988.
The American Controversy: A Bibliographical Study of the British Pamphlets about the American Disputes, 1764–1783. 2 vols. By Thomas R. Adams. Providence: Brown UP, 1980.

Early American Music Engraving and Printing: A History of Music Publishing in America from 1787 to 1825 with Commentary on Earlier and Later Practices. By Richard J. Wolfe. Urbana: U of Illinois P, 1980.

The society is also supervising publication of the *Bibliography of American Literature.*

The annual meeting is held each January in New York.

BSA awards fellowships to support bibliographical inquiry and research in the history of publishing and the book trades.

BSA is a constituent society of ACLS.

65.   Bibliographical Society of Canada/Société Bibliographique du Canada (BSC/SBC)
PO Box 575, Postal Station P
Toronto, ON M5S 2T1, Canada
Founded 1946
375 members
Secretary: Liana Van Der Bellen
The principal aims of the society are to promote bibliographical publications; to encourage the preservation and to extend the knowledge of printed works and manuscripts, particularly those relating to Canada; to facilitate the exchange of information concerning rare Canadiana; to coordinate bibliographical activity and to set standards.

Periodicals
Papers/Cahiers. Ed. Bruce Whiteman (McGill Univ.). Annual. Features scholarly articles in French and English on all aspects of bibliography, including printing, publishing, and textual studies.
Bulletin. Ed. Martin Dowding. Semiannual newsletter.

BSC/SBC holds an annual meeting in May or June. The special topic of the 1989 meeting, held in Edmonton, AB, was Bibliography and Computers.

The Marie Tremaine Medal is awarded for outstanding service to Canadian bibliography and for a distinguished publication in French or English in that field. Tremaine Fellowships assist members engaged in bibliographical research.

66.   Canadian Association of Slavists (CAS)
Department of Slavic Languages and Literatures
21 Sussex Avenue
University of Toronto
Toronto, ON M5S 1A1, Canada
Founded 1954
450 members
Tel. 416 978-4895
Secretary-Treasurer: Kenneth Lantz
The association seeks to promote and advance of Slavic studies in Canada.

Periodicals
Canadian Slavonic Papers. Ed. Wayne Dowler. Quarterly.
Newsletter. Ed. Kenneth Lantz. Biannual.

CAS holds an annual meeting each June; the 1990 meeting will be held in Victoria, BC.

67. Canadian Linguistic Association/Association Canadienne de Linguistique (CLA/ACL)
Département de Linguistique
Université du Québec à Montréal
CP 8888, succursale A
Montréal, PQ H3C 3P8, Canada
Founded 1954
650 members
Tel. 416 978-3162
Secretary-Treasurer: Paul Pupier
CLA/ACL is a scholarly and professional society composed largely of professors and graduate students of linguistics. The association has one essential purpose: to foster the study of linguistics and language in Canada.

Periodicals
Canadian Journal of Linguistics/La revue canadienne de linguistique. Ed. William Cowan (Dept. of Linguistics, Carleton Univ., Ottowa, ON K1S 5B6, Canada). Quarterly. Bilingual.
Bulletin of the Canadian Linguistic Association. Ed. Paul Pupier. Annual.

CLA/ACL holds an annual conference in conjunction with the meeting of the Learned Societies of Canada, at which members present original research papers.

68. Children's Literature Association (ChLA)
Department of English
University of Winnipeg
Winnipeg, AB R3B 2E9, Canada
Founded 1973
800 members
Tel. 204 786-9261
Secretary: Perry Nodleman
The object of the association is to encourage scholarship, research, and literary criticism in the field of children's literature and to enhance the professional stature of the undergraduate and graduate teaching of children's literature and the teaching of literature to children.

Periodicals
Children's Literature Association Quarterly. Ed. Roderick McGillis. Features juried articles about research and scholarship in children's literature, special sections devoted to particular topics, and announcements.
Children's Literature. Ed. Francelia Butler. Annual. Includes articles on various authors, illustrators, and periods of children's literature, as well as interpretive essays and book reviews.
The ChLA Conference Proceedings. Annual.

Publications

Touchstones: Reflections on the Best in Children's Literature. 3 vols. Ed. Perry Nodleman. 1985, 1986, 1987.

Graduate Studies in Children's Literature.

The First Steps: Best of the Early ChLA Quarterly. Ed. Patricia Dooley. 1985.

Children and Their Literature: A Readings Book. Ed. Jill P. May. 1983.

Literary Criticism, Children and Teachers: A Booklist. 1985.

In addition to its annual meeting each May, ChLA sponsors sessions at the MLA convention. ChLA's 1990 meeting, Work and Play, will be held in San Diego, CA.

ChLA annually sponsors the Phoenix Award for the most outstanding book published twenty years ago that did not receive an award at the time, awards for the most significant scholarly or critical article and book about children's literature, and a prize for the best critical article written by a teenager about children's literature.

The association sponsors workshops on teaching literary criticism to children in kindergarten through eighth grade.

69. **Chinese Language Teachers Association (CLTA)**
     Institute of Far Eastern Studies
     Seton Hall University
     South Orange, NJ 07079
Founded 1962
500 members
Tel. 201 761-9447/762-4973
Secretary-Treasurer: John Young

The association strives to improve the professional status of Chinese language teachers, to develop general standards for the teaching of Chinese, to prepare standardized tests, and to promote the teaching of Chinese in colleges and high schools. Members include scholars, teachers, and students in the fields of Chinese language, linguistics, literature, and related areas.

Periodicals

Journal of the Chinese Language Teachers Association. Ed. James Tai (Ohio State Univ.). Pub. 3 times a year.

CLTA Newsletter. Pub. 3 times a year. Professional developments and placement information.

CLTA holds annual meetings in conjunction with the national conventions of the MLA, the Association for Asian Studies (AAS), and ACTFL.

70. **Classical Association of the Pacific Northwest (CAPN)**
     Department of Foreign Languages
     University of Montana
     Missoula, MT 59812
Founded 1970
125 members
Tel. 406 243-2541
Secretary-Treasurer: John D. Madden

CAPN promotes the study of the classics at all educational levels, from elementary school through university, cooperates with other organizations of similar purpose, and provides a forum for high school and university teachers in the region to meet and exchange ideas on matters of pedagogy and critical research in all disciplines having to do with classical antiquity.

Periodical: *CAPN Bulletin*. Ed. Ili Nagy (Dept. of Art, Univ. of Puget Sound, Tacoma, WA 98416). Pub. Oct. and Feb.

CAPN meets each spring. The 1990 meeting will be held at Reed College in Portland, OR. (For further information, write Walter Englert, Dept. of Classics, Reed Coll., Portland, OR 97202).

The association sponsors grants for instructional materials and travel scholarships for high school teachers and graduate students in classics.

71. College Art Association (CAA)
275 7th Avenue
New York, NY 10001
Founded 1913
10,000 members
Tel. 212 691-1051
Executive Director: Susan Ball
The association's purpose is to further scholarship and excellence in the teaching and practice of art and art history. Its membership comprises scholars, teachers, artists, critics, museum professionals, art dealers and collectors, and art and slide librarians.

Periodicals
Art Bulletin. Ed. Walter Cohen. Quarterly. Scholarly articles and reviews of books in all periods of art history.
Art Journal. Guest editor each issue. Quarterly. Ideas and opinions that focus on critical and aesthetic issues, primarily in modern art.
CAA Newsletter. Quarterly.

The Millard Weiss Publication Fund subsidizes the publication of book-length scholarly manuscripts that have been accepted by a publisher but cannot be published without a subsidy. The association publishes directories of fine arts and art history programs and other reference works.

Meetings
1990: 14–17 Feb., New York, NY
1991: 20–23 Feb., Washington, DC
1992: 12–15 Feb., Chicago, IL
1993: 3–6 Feb., Seattle, WA
1994: 25–29 Jan., New York, NY

The association provides a placement service at the annual meeting and mails its *Positions Listings* — including openings at museums, galleries, and art publishers, as well as teaching positions — six times a year.

Prizes awarded
Distinguished Teaching of Art Award
Distinguished Teaching of Art History Award
Distinguished Artist Award for lifetime achievement
Artist Award for a distinguished body of work, exhibition, presentation, or performance
Alfred H. Barr, Jr., Award for a distinguished catalog in the history of art
Charles Rufus Morey Book Award for an outstanding book in art history
Arthur Kingsley Porter Prize for an outstanding article in the *Art Bulletin*
Frank Jewett Mather Award for excellence in art or architectural criticism

CAA administers the *Reader's Digest* Artists at Giverny Program, which provides funds for artists to live and work in Giverny, France, the home of Claude Monet.

CAA is a constituent member of the American Arts Alliance, the American Council on the Arts, ACLS, and NHA.

72.   College English Association (CEA)
Department of English
Nazareth College of Rochester
Rochester, New York 14610
Founded 1939
1,500 members
Tel. 716 586-2525
Executive Director: John J. Joyce
CEA is a national organization of teacher-scholars who regard the instruction of students, undergraduate and graduate, as the proper focus of the profession. The annual meetings, the work of the standing and ad hoc committees, and all other activities are devoted to supporting the work of classroom teachers in their professional pursuits. Members represent a broad range of interests traditionally gathered under the umbrella of "English." These interests include literature, language, linguistics, composition, creative writing, women's and minority studies, journalism, technical communication, speech, American studies, ESL, and popular culture.

CEA Critic reflects the energy, variety, and discoveries of current research in English literature and language, particularly as it applies in the classroom, aiming to provide as complete a picture as possible of the wide range of scholarship now occurring in the discipline. *CEA Forum* features information and opinions on the state of the profession, airing critical problems and possible solutions. Both journals are published quarterly and edited by Barbara Brothers and Bege Bowers (English Dept., Youngstown State Univ., Youngstown, OH 44555).

Chapbooks, focussing on classroom needs, and *A Directory of College and University Writing Programs* are published on an irregular basis.

Meetings
        1990: 5–7 Apr., Buffalo, NY
        1991: 17–19 Apr., San Antonio, TX

The association annually sponsors the $500 Robert Hacke Award for research work by a younger CEA member in English studies.

CEA supports the work of twenty regional affiliates throughout the contiguous United States and Puerto Rico. These affiliates have one or two yearly meetings of their own and publish newsletters or journals.

73.   College Language Association (CLA)
        Clark Atlanta University
        Atlanta, GA 30314
Founded 1937
700 members
Tel. 404 880-8524/8525
Secretary: Lucy C. Grigsby
CLA is an organization of college teachers of English and foreign languages that serves the academic, scholarly, and professional interests of its members and the collegiate communities they represent. Included in its objectives are improving the study and teaching of language skills, cultivating appreciation of language and literature, and encouraging scholarly research in and teaching of black literatures and cultures as necessary aspects of higher education.

Periodical: *CLA Journal.* Ed. Cason Hill (Morehouse Coll., Atlanta, GA 30314). Quarterly.

CLA holds its annual convention each April; in 1989, the theme of the Frankfurt, KY, meeting was Culture and Literacy: The Role of Language, Literature, and Linguistics. The theme of the 1990 meeting, to be held in Columbus, OH, will be Shaping and Reshaping Culture: Forces in Literature and Language. The Langston Hughes Society, an affiliate of CLA, usually sponsors a session at the convention. In addition, CLA is affiliated with the MLA, NCTE, and CCCC, and sponsors a session at each of their annual conventions.

CLA operates a placement bureau at its Atlanta University office.

CLA sponsors an award for the most distinguished contribution (book or article) to literary or linguistic scholarship by a member.

Individual members are available as consultants in humanistic disciplines for colleges, universities, and schools. The association has also worked to enhance humanities programs in the Washington, DC, public schools.

CLA participates in the work of the National English Coalition.

74.   Computer Assisted Language Learning and Instruction Consortium (CALICO)
        3078 JKHB
        Brigham Young University
        Provo, UT 84602
Founded 1983
1,200 members
Tel. 801 378-7079
Executive Director: Frank Otto
CALICO serves as an international clearinghouse and leader in computer-assisted language instruction. The consortium includes leaders, innovators, and well-known experts from all areas of computer-assisted language learning, including all levels

of education, business, government, research, and manufacturing. Members may become involved in one or more of the following special interest groups: Artificial Intelligence, CD-ROM, Computers in the Classroom, Courseware Development, Foreign Character Fonts/Asian Languages, Hypermedia, Infowindow System, and Interactive Audio/Video.

Periodical: *CALICO Journal*. Ed. Frank Otto. Quarterly. Includes articles on the concerns and problems of this rapidly growing field, courseware reviews, product information, and a calender of technology-related conferences.

The first two volumes in the CALICO Monograph Series are *Applications of Technology: Planning and Using Language Learning Centers* and *Interactive Video: The How and Why*. CALICO also produces informational videotapes designed to help educators understand the advantages and disadvantages of various technologies.

The annual symposium brings together educators, administrators, materials developers, researchers, government representatives, hardware and software vendors, and other interested persons to participate in a forum for discussing state-of-the-art technology in a variety of disciplines. Activities include hands-on seminars, exhibits, demonstrations, and panel discussions.
      1990: 19–23 Mar., Baltimore, MD

Since 1988, CALICO has sponsored an annual satellite teleconference. Topics have included Emerging Technologies in Modern Language Instruction and Using Technology in the Modern Language Classroom.

Regional seminars held at sites throughout the United States and Canada provide educators with practical instruction in technology.
   CALICO's summer institute provides an opportunity for novices and experienced users to increase their insight and skills in the applications of computer-assisted language instruction. Topics range from materials development to administration of programs.

75.   Conference on Christianity and Literature (CCL)
      University of Southern Mississippi
      Southern Station Box 10055
      Hattiesburg, MS 39406
Founded 1956
1,200 members
Tel. 601 266-5828
President: James H. Sims
CCL is an international society of professionals dedicated to a growing awareness and understanding of the relations between Christianity and the creation, study, and teaching of literature.

Periodical: *Christianity and Literature*. Ed. Robert Snyder (Seattle Pacific Univ., Seattle, WA 98119). Quarterly. Contains articles devoted to the scholarly exploration of how literature engages Christian thought, experience, and practice; also publishes review essays, poetry, book reviews, and news items.

As an allied organization of the MLA, CCL sponsors programs at each MLA convention. The 1988 program addressed the topic of T. S. Eliot and the Scriptural Tradition and featured a reading by Wendell Berry; Christian Criticism: Can/Should It Exist? and Centenary Perspectives on Gerard Manley Hopkins were discussed in 1989. In addition, each of the nine regional associations holds an annual conference.

The society awards a citation to the author of the CCL Book of the Year for a work that "has contributed most to the dialogue between literature and the Christian Faith" and sponsors a student writing contest for essays, poems, and stories that discuss or reflect Christian themes in life or literature.

76. Council on National Literatures (CNL)
PO Box 81
Whitestone, NY 11357
Founded 1974
1,000 members
Tel. 718 767-8380
President: Anne Paolucci

The council aims to expand comparative literary study into areas not currently in the European or "Western" mainstream—Yugoslav, Turkish, Greek, Armenian, and Australian literatures, for example—through publications devoted to such literatures; it also seeks to open dialogue among members on issues pertaining to the expansion of comparative literature into multinational areas.

Periodicals
Review of National Literatures. Annual. Each issue focuses on a national culture or representative theme, author, literary movement, or critical tendency, in an effort to provide substantial and concentrated critical materials for comparative studies of Western and non-Western literatures.
CNL/World Report. Annual. Proceedings of annual and special meetings.
CNL/Review of Books. Pub. 6 times a year.

Occasional special issues of books are published through Griffon House.

As an allied organization of the MLA, CNL usually sponsors sessions at the annual convention; the topic in 1989 was Literary Academic Journals in the Mainstream.

77. Economic History Association (EHA)
Department of History
George Washington University
Washington, DC 20052
Founded 1940
3,200 members
Tel. 202 994-6052
Secretary-Treasurer: William H. Becker

The association's purposes are to stimulate interest in the study of economic history; to encourage research in economic history and ideas; to cooperate with societies devoted to the study of agricultural, industrial, technological, or business history; and to collaborate with economists, historians, statisticians, geographers, and all other students of economic change.

Periodical: *Journal of Economic History.* Ed. Paul Hohenberg and Thomas Weiss. Quarterly.

Meeting: 1990: 13–16 Sept., Montreal, PQ

The association sponsors prizes in economic history for mature scholars and doctoral students.

EHA is a member of the International Economic History Association and a constituent member of ACLS.

78.   Esperanto Studies Association of America (ESAA)
        749 East Beaumont Avenue
        Whitefish Bay, WI 53217
Founded 1975
67 members
Tel. 414 962-9556
Secretary-Treasurer: Pierre L. Ullman

The association's purpose is to advance the scholarly study of Esperanto and related aspects of language problems and interlinguistics by bringing specialists in Esperanto studies together at an annual symposium, by informing such specialists of new developments in the field, by encouraging research in progress, by promoting the exchange of ideas in Esperanto studies nationally and internationally, and by working to improve the holdings of books in and on Esperanto in American libraries.

ESAA publishes an occasional news bulletin.

The association meets each year at the MLA convention.

79.   Gay and Lesbian Caucus for the Modern Languages (GLCML)
        PO Box 415
        Kittery, ME 03904
Founded 1972
275 members
Secretary: Jack Yeager

The caucus promotes research on gay and lesbian literary concerns and combats homophobia within the profession of language and literatures. Largely as a result of the caucus's efforts, the legitimacy of gay studies was recognized by the MLA when it incorporated a new Division on Gay Studies in Language and Literature; the division held its first sessions at the 1981 MLA convention. While there is some overlap, the division, as an official part of the MLA, organizes sessions on scholarly research into lesbian and gay language and literature and functions within the MLA itself to represent the concerns of its members. The caucus, while also devoted to advancing research, is concerned with investigating the effects of homophobia in the profession and with actively assisting gay and lesbian scholars in their struggle for academic acceptance. Both publicly, through the caucus's newsletter, and privately, through correspondence, the caucus distributes information about lesbian and gay issues to academics around the country.

Periodical: *Gay Studies Newsletter.* Ed. Michael Lynch (Dept. of English, Univ. of Toronto, Toronto, ON M5S 1A1, Canada). Pub. 3 times a year. In addition to reporting on caucus activities and the MLA convention, *GSN* includes book reviews, news items relevant to lesbian and gay academics, bibliographies, and other announcements.

The caucus meets once a year at the MLA convention, where it sponsors two sessions.

The caucus confers the Compton-Noll Award for the best published or unpublished essay on a topic related to gay studies in literature.

The caucus has a liaison with the MLA's Commission on the Status of Women to ensure that the special concerns of lesbians are considered.

80.   History of Science Society (HSS)

35 Dean Street
Worcester, MA 01609
Founded 1924
2,950 members; 1,600 institutional
Tel. 508 793-0712
Executive Secretary: Michael M. Sokhal

HSS is the world's largest organization dedicated to understanding science, technology, and medicine and the social and cultural relations of these fields. The society seeks to advance research and teaching in the history of science — from prehistoric times to the present, from the astronomical observations of the ancient precivilizations to the impact of modern science on technology, medicine, religion, education, and government. The society and its publications provide both the public at large and decision makers with historical perspectives on science policy and on the achievements, potentials, and limitations of all forms of scientific thought and practice.

Periodicals

Isis. Ed. Ronald L. Numbers (Univ. of Wisconsin). Quarterly. Includes editorials, scholarly and review articles, research notes, documentation, book reviews, and professional news.

Current Bibliography of the History of Science. Ed. John Neu (Univ. of Wisconsin). Annual. Indexes the entire literature of the discipline.

Osiris. Ed. Arnold Thackery (Univ. of Pennsylvania). Annual. Each volume provides state-of-the-art analysis and review of a different major theme in the history of science.

Newsletter. Ed. Michael Sokal (Worcester Polytechnic Inst.). Quarterly. Includes professional news and employment opportunities.

Guide to the History of Science. Ed. P. Thomas Carroll (Rensselaer Polytechnic Inst.). Pub. every 3 years. Includes membership directory; guides to graduate study and research, to scholarly journals, and to societies and other organizations; and a list of booksellers.

Isis Critical Bibliography. Annual.

Cumulative bibliographies of *Isis* are available for 1913–65, 1966–75, and 1976–85. *The Dictionary of Scientific Biography* is published by Charles Scribner's Sons under the auspices of ACLS, with the cooperation of HSS.

The society convenes once each year. In addition, HSS attempts to meet once every four years in congress with the Philosophy of Science Association, the Society for the History of Technology (see SHOT), and the Society for Social Studies of Science (most recently in 1986); and every four years with the American Historical Association (most recently in 1988).

> 1990: 25–28 Oct., Seattle, WA
> 1991: 31 Oct.–3 Nov., Madison, WI

Prizes awarded

Sarton Medal for a distinguished career in the history of science

Henry and Ida Schuman Prize for the best essay on the history of science by a graduate student

Pfizer Award for the best book on the history of science by an American or Canadian author

Derek Price Award (formerly the Zeitlin–Ver Brugge Prize) for an outstanding article in *Isis*

Watson Davis Prize for the best book used in teaching or promoting the history of science

Prize for the History of Women in Science for the best book or (in alternate years) article in this area of specialization

The Independent Scholars Program provides small grants for individuals who are educated in the field or doing research in it and who are unemployed, unaffiliated with any institution making use of their training and experience, or employed either part-time or without prospect of renewal. The Visiting Historians of Science Program provides partial support for bringing leading scholars before audiences at colleges and universities at which the discipline is not currently represented. The Thematic Meetings Program endorses or provides partial support for conferences of scholarly merit that serve diverse audiences and regional needs not met by the HSS annual meeting.

The History of Science Society Distinguished Lecture is presented at the society's annual meeting. The George Sarton Memorial Lecture, supported jointly by HSS and the American Association for the Advancement of Science, is delivered by a leading historian of science at the AAAS's annual meeting.

HSS is a constituent member of ACLS and has representation on the United States National Committee for the International Union of the History and Philosophy of Science. It is an affiliate of AAAS and participates in the Consortium of Social Science Associations, NHA, and the National Coordinating Committee for the Promotion of History.

81.   International Arthurian Society, North American Branch (IAS/NAB)
Department of French
Dalhousie University
Halifax, NS B3H 3J5, Canada
Founded 1948
400 members
Tel. 902 424-2430
Secretary-Treasurer: H. R. Runte

The purpose of the society is to further the study of Arthurian, medieval romance, and related literatures, especially by sharing knowledge at the triennial international congresses and by publishing research.

Periodicals
Bibliographical Bulletin of the International Arthurian Society. Ed. Douglas Kelly. Annual.
IAS/NAB Newsletter. Ed. Hans R. Runte. Biannual.

The society's twelve branches hold an international congress every three years; the next congress will be held at Durham University, England, in 1990. The North American branch holds an annual meeting in May, in conjunction with the International Congress on Medieval Studies organized by the Medieval Institute of Western Michigan University, Kalamazoo.

82.   International Reading Association (IRA)
    800 Barksdale Road
    PO Box 8139
    Newark, DE 19174-8139
Founded 1956
90,000 members
Tel. 302 731-1600
Executive Director: Ronald W. Mitchell
IRA has three general goals: to improve the quality of reading instruction through the study of the reading process and of teaching techniques; to promote the habit of lifetime reading and the public's awareness of the impact of reading; and to promote the development of every reader's proficiency to the highest level.

Periodicals
The Reading Teacher. Pub. 8 times a year. Directed toward elementary school educators.
Journal of Reading. Pub. 8 times a year. Concerned with teaching reading at secondary, college, and adult levels.
Reading Research Quarterly. Technically oriented for those interested in reading research.
Lectura y Vida. Spanish-language quarterly edited in Latin America.
Reading Today. Bimonthly newspaper. News and features about the reading profession.

The association has in print approximately 150 publications on reading and related topics, including reports, bibliographies, critical collections, special studies, and teacher aids.

IRA holds an annual convention, a number of regional conferences, and, biennially, a world conference at a site outside North America. The next world conference will be held in Stockholm, Sweden, 3–6 July 1990.
    1990: 6–10 May, Atlanta, GA
    1991: 6–10 May, Las Vegas, NV

Job placement services are offered at the annual convention, and members may subscribe to a monthly placement newsletter.

IRA sponsors the International Literacy Award, presented on International Literacy Day by UNESCO for outstanding work in the promotion of literacy. The association also presents awards at the annual convention for teaching, service to the profession, an outstanding dissertation, research, media coverage of reading, and children's-book writing.

IRA awards the Institute for Reading Research Fellowship to a researcher outside the United States or Canada who has received the PhD or its equivalent within the past five years and evidences exceptional promise in reading research.

More than sixty volunteer committees explore such areas as computer technology and reading, early childhood and literacy development, teacher education and effectiveness, multiliteracy in multicultural settings, and adult literacy.

83.   International Society for General Semantics (ISGS)
PO Box 2469
San Francisco, CA 94126
Founded 1943
2,300 members
Tel. 415 543-1749
Executive Director: Russell Joyner
ISGS seeks to explore the ways language shapes society and our image of ourselves and others, to uncover the limitations and rigidities of language, and to improve the ability of to think critically.

Periodicals
Et cetera. Ed. Russell Joyner. Quarterly. Devoted to the role of language and symbols in human behavior.
Glimpse. Ed. Russell Joyner. Quarterly newsletter.

Publications
The Language of Wisdom and Folly. Ed. Irving J. Lee.
Words, Meanings, People. By Sanford I. Berman.
Communications: The Transfer of Meaning. By Don Fabun.
Teaching General Semantics. Ed. Mary Morain.

ISGS sponsors the Sanford I. Berman Research Scholarships in General Semantics.

84.   Latin American Studies Association (LASA)
LASA Secretariat
William Pitt Union, 9th Floor
University of Pittsburgh
Pittsburgh, PA 15260
Founded 1966
2,600 members
Tel. 412 648-7929
Executive Director: Reid Reading
LASA fosters the interests of scholars of Latin American studies; encourages more effective training, teaching, and research in connection with such studies; and provides a forum for addressing matters of common interest to scholars and other individuals concerned with Latin American studies.

Periodicals
Latin American Research Review. Ed. Gilbert Merkx (Univ. of New Mexico). Pub.
　3 times a year.
LASA Forum. Quarterly. Includes brief research-based articles and announcements
　of employment, research, and travel opportunities.

Publications
Latin American Education: A Quest for Identity. Sponsored by the Consortium of Latin
　American Studies Programs (CLASP). By Nancy J. Nystrom. 1986.
Peace and Autonomy on the Atlantic Coast of Nicaragua. By the LASA Task Force on
　Human Rights and Academic Freedom, Martin Diskin, Thomas Bossert,
　Salomón Nahmad, and Stefano Varese. 1986.
*Final Report of the LASA Commission on Compliance with the Central American Peace
　Accords*. Mar. 1988.
The Chilean Plebiscite: A First Step toward Redemocratization. By the International Com-
　mission of LASA to Observe the Chilean Plebiscite. 1989.

International conferences are held every eighteen months. At the 1989 conference, held 21–23 September in San Juan, PR, topics included issues of particular
significance to Puerto Rico and the Caribbean: race and ethnicity, cultural minorities and the national question, and critical public policy issues. The 1991 conference will be held in Washington, DC.

A media award for outstanding coverage of Latin American topics and an award
for the outstanding book on Latin America in the humanities and social sciences
published in English in the United States are awarded at the International
Congress.

The Consortium of Latin American Studies Programs (CLASP) is the institutional affiliate of LASA. Formed in the fall of 1968, it seeks to promote the cause
of Latin American studies and to act on matters of interest and value to institutional members, except in areas where other LASA organs have responsibility.

LASA currently supports task forces on human rights and academic freedom;
on scholarly relations with Central America, Nicaragua, Cuba, the Soviet Union,
and Spain; on women in Latin American studies, and on mass media.

85.　Linguistic Society of America (LSA)
　　　1325 18th Street, NW
　　　Suite 211
　　　Washington, DC 20036-6501
Founded 1924
7,000 members
Tel. 202 835-1714
Secretary-Treasurer: Frederick J. Newmeyer
The association promotes research and publication in the scientific analysis of
language and literature.

Periodicals
Language. Ed. Sarah G. Thompson. Quarterly. Technical articles on linguistic
　science and reviews of recently published works.
LSA Bulletin. Quarterly. News and announcements of interest to the profession.

Publications
Directory of Programs in Linguistics in the United States and Canada. Updated every 3 years.
Guide to Grants and Fellowships in Linguistics 1988–90. Updated every 3 years.
Handbook for Grant Proposal Preparation. 1986.
The Field of Linguistics. 1985.

Meeting: 1990: 3–6 Jan., Chicago, IL

Linguistic institutes are held biannually, in odd-numbered years at institutions around the United States. The 1989 institute — Bridges: Cross-Linguistic, Cross-Cultural, and Cross-Disciplinary Approaches to Language — was cosponsored by the MLA and was held 26 June–4 August at the University of Arizona, Tucson. The 1991 institute will be hosted by the University of California, Santa Cruz. Fellowships are awarded to qualified student attendees.

LSA is a constituent member of ACLS, JNCL/CLOIS, NHA, and the Consortium of Social Science Associations.

86. **Lyrica Society for Word-Music Relations (LYRICA)**
     90 Church Street
     Guilford, CT 06437
Founded 1979
250 members
Tel. 203 453-1503
Secretary-Treasurer: Louis E. Auld
LYRICA promotes and encourages activity and research related to the association of words and music of any sort.

Periodicals
Ars LYRICA. Ed. Louis E. Auld. Annual.
LYRICA Newsletter. Semiannual.

Publication: Burning Bright: *Genesis of an Opera.* Interview of Frank Lewin by Lewis E. Auld. 1986.

LYRICA sponsors two sessions at the annual MLA Convention.

87. **Marxist Literary Group (MLG)**
     Department of French and Italian
     248 Cunz Hall
     Ohio State University
     Columbus, OH 43210-1229
Founded 1975
400 members
Tel. 614 292-4838
Secretary-Treasurer: Eugene W. Holland
MLG provides a network for various regional, national, and international activities broadly concerned with Marxist perspectives on culture. Principal permanent activities include organizing sessions for the annual MLA and regional MLA conventions, sponsoring the annual Summer Institute for Culture and Society, and producing the newsletter *Mediations.* Other occasional activities include produc-

tion and dissemination of bibliographies, organization of local reading groups and seminars, and participation in other projects proposed by members.

Periodical: *Mediations.* Ed. Walter Cohen (Comparative Literature, Cornell Univ., Ithaca, NY 14853). Semiannual.

88. Medieval Academy of America
   1430 Massachusetts Avenue
   Cambridge, MA 02138
Founded 1925
3,625 members
Tel. 617 491-1622
Executive Director: Luke Wenger
The Medieval Academy of America promotes research, publication, and instruction in medieval records, art, archaeology, history, law, literature, music, philosophy, science, social and economic institutions, and all other aspects of the Middle Ages. Membership is open to anyone interested in the Middle Ages.

Periodicals
Speculum: A Journal of Medieval Studies. Ed. Luke Wenger. Quarterly.
Medieval Academy News. Pub. 3 times a year. Includes job listings.

Publications
Gothic Art, 1140–1450. By Teresa G. Frisch. Reprints for Teaching. Downsview, ON: U of Toronto P.
Byzantium: The Imperial Centuries, AD 610–1071. By Romilly Jenkins. Reprints for Teaching. Downsview, ON: U of Toronto P.
The Discovery of the Individual, 1050–1200. By Colin Morris. Reprints for Teaching. Downsview, ON: U of Toronto P.
Averroes' "De substantia orbis". Ed. and trans. Arthur Hyman. 1986.
Petrarch's "Secretum": Its Making and Its Meaning. By Hans Baron. 1985.
Wilhelm Jordaen's "Avellana": A Fourteenth-Century Virtue-Vice Debate. Ed. Lawrence J. Johnson. 1985.
Truth and Scientific Knowledge in the Thought of Henry of Ghent. By Steven P. Marrone. 1985.
The "Cansos" of Raimon de Miraval: A Study of Poems and Melodies. By Margaret Louise Switten. 1985.
Alan of Lille's Grammar of Sex: The Meaning of Grammar to a Twelfth-Century Intellectual. By Jan Ziolkowski. 1985.

Meetings
   1990: 5–7 Apr., Vancouver, BC
   1991: Apr., Princeton, NJ
   1992: Apr., Columbus, OH

Prizes awarded
Haskins Medal for a distinguished book in medieval studies
John Nicholas Brown Prize for a first book in medieval studies
Elliott Prize for a first article in medieval studies

The academy is a constituent member of ACLS and is affiliated with the Association International des Etudes Byzantines.

89.   **Middle East Studies Association of North America (MESA)**
      1232 North Cherry Avenue
      University of Arizona
      Tucson, AZ 85721
Founded 1964
2,000 members
Tel. 602 621-5850
Executive Secretary: Michael E. Bonine
MESA is an academic, nonpolitical organization for those with scholarly train-
ing and interest in Middle East studies.

Periodicals
International Journal of Middle Eastern Studies. Ed. Leila Fawaz (Tufts Univ.).
      Quarterly.
MESA Bulletin. Ed. Jere Bacharach (Univ. of Washington). Semiannual.
MESA Newsletter. Ed. Wendy Wiener (Univ. of Arizona). Quarterly.

MESA publishes a *Directory of Graduate and Undergraduate Programs and Courses in
Middle East Studies in the United States, Canada, and Abroad* every other year. It also
produces teaching materials and resources through the Middle East Outreach
Council.

MESA's twenty-two affiliates hold meetings and cosponsor panels and discussions
at the MESA annual meeting in addition to their own approximately ninety regular
sessions and events.
      1990: 10–13 Nov., San Antonio, TX
      1991: Washington, DC

The annual Malcolm H. Kerr Dissertation Awards honor the best dissertation
in the humanities and the best dissertation in the social sciences.

Through its Visiting Scholars Program, MESA invites one distinguished scholar
or more from Europe or the Middle East to give lectures at institutions in the
United States.

MESA is a constituent member of ACLS.

90.   **Midwest Modern Language Association (MMLA)**
      302 English-Philosophy Building
      University of Iowa
      Iowa City, IA 52242-1408
Founded 1959
2,000 members
Tel. 319 335-0331
Executive Director: Maria A. Duarte
The MMLA has as its objective the advancement of criticism, research, and teaching in the modern languages and literatures. Membership is primarily though
not exclusively drawn from the states of Illinois, Iowa, Kansas, Michigan, Minnesota, Nebraska, North Dakota, Ohio, South Dakota, and Wisconsin.

Periodical: *The Journal of the Midwest Modern Language Association.* Ed. Maria A.
Duarte. Pub. May and Sept. Contains essays on the teaching of language and

literature, particularly in relation to political, historical, and cultural issues, critical methodology, literary history, and theory of language.

Publication: *The Horizon of Literature*. Ed. Paul Hernadi. Lincoln: U of Nebraska P, 1982.

Meetings
>1990: 1–3 Nov., Kansas City, MO
>1991: 14–16 Nov., Chicago, IL

MMLA is a regional affiliate of the MLA.

91.   Modern Greek Studies Association (MGSA)
>Box 1826
>New Haven, CT 06508

Founded 1968
450 members
Tel. 203 397-4189
Executive Director: John O. Iatrides

MGSA promotes the study of modern Greece, particularly in the United States and Canada but also wherever interest exists and support is needed. Interdisciplinary in orientation, the association seeks to stimulate the discovery and diffusion of knowledge about the language, arts, history, politics, economy, and society of modern Greece. MGSA's scope includes not only postindependence Greece but also the period of Ottoman rule and the later Byzantine Empire, as well as those aspects of Byzantine, Hellenistic, and classical times that have a bearing on the modern period.

Periodicals
Journal of Modern Greek Studies. Ed. Ernestine Friedl. Semiannual.
MGSA Bulletin. Ed. John O. Iatrides. Semiannual.

Publications
Greece in the 1940's: A Nation in Crisis. Ed. John O. Iatrides. Hanover: UP of New
>England, 1981.
Greece in the 1940's: A Bibliographic Companion. Ed. John O. Iatrides. Hanover: UP
>of New England, 1981.
New Trends in Modern Greek Historiography. MGSA Occasional Paper 1. By A. Lily
>Macrakis and P. Nikiforos Diamandouros. 1982.

A bibliographic project on modern Greece is currently in progress.

About every two years, MGSA sponsors a symposium. The 1989 symposium, Power/Freedom: Politics, Social Life, and the Arts in Modern Greece, took place at the University of Minnesota, Minneapolis.

The association maintains an informal placement service.

Summer seminars are held in Greece at irregular intervals.

To promote access to information and to provide for jointly sponsored meetings focusing on shared themes, MGSA has become affiliated with other professional organizations, including AAASS, ACTFL, AHA, APA (the American Philological Association), the MLA, and the International Studies Association.

92.   Modern Humanities Research Association, American Branch (MHRA)

Columbian College
George Washington University
Washington, DC 20052
Founded 1918
700 members worldwide
Tel. 202 994-6963
American Secretary: Calvin D. Linton

The association encourages and promotes advanced study and research in the field of modern humanities, especially modern European languages and literatures, including English. Major concerns are to break down the barriers among scholars working in different disciplines and to maintain the broader unity of humanistic scholarship in the face of increasing specialization. MHRA attempts to fulfill this purpose by publishing journals, bibliographies, monographs, and other aids to research; providing assistance toward the publication of original work; arranging individual contacts between scholars; and offering advice and help to those visiting countries other than their own.

Periodicals

The Modern Language Review. Quarterly.
Yearbook of English Studies. Annual.
The Year's Work in English Studies. Annual.
Annual Bibliography of English Language and Literature.
The Slavonic and East European Review. Annual.
Portuguese Studies. Annual.
Annual Bulletin of the Modern Humanities Research Association.

Publications

Myth and Legend in French Literature: Essays in Honour of A. J. Steele. Publications of the MHRA. By Keith Aspley, David Bellos, and Peter Sharratt. 1982.
Book Production and Letters in the Western European Renaissance: Essays in Honour of Conor Fahy. Publications of the MHRA. By Anna Laura Lepschy, John Took, and Dennis E. Rhodes. 1986.
The Second Continuation of the Old French Perceval. MHRA Texts and Dissertations 24. By Corin F. Corley. 1987.
Quevedo on Parnassus: Allusive Context and Literary Theory in the Love-Lyric. MHRA Texts and Dissertations 25. By Paul Julian Smith. 1987.

The American branch of MHRA meets in conjunction with the MLA annual convention. The meeting of the entire MHRA is held each January, usually in London, England.

MHRA is an affiliated member organization of the International Federation for Modern Languages and Literatures sponsored by UNESCO.

93.   Modern Language Association of America (MLA)

10 Astor Place
New York, NY 10003-6981
Founded 1883
25,000 members
Tel. 212 475-9500

Executive Director: Phyllis Franklin

The association promotes "study, criticism, and research in the more and less commonly taught languages and their literatures and furthers the common interests of teachers of these subjects." To fulfill these goals, the MLA arranges an annual convention and other meetings for its members, publishes scholarly and professional journals and books, compiles an annual bibliography of the modern languages and their literatures, conducts surveys of English and foreign language departments, houses ADE and ADFL (see listings), maintains a job service for members, and carries out special projects.

Members include students, teachers, and scholars of the modern languages and their literatures. They may participate in the 109 discussion groups and divisions of specialized scholarly and professional interest.

Periodicals

PMLA (*Publications of the Modern Language Association*). Ed. John Kronik. Pub. 6 times a year; Sept. issue is directory of members and Nov. issue serves as convention program.

Profession. Ed. Phyllis Franklin. Annual. Includes reprints from *ADE Bulletin* and *ADFL Bulletin* and original essays of general professional interest.

MLA Newsletter. Ed. Phyllis Franklin. Quarterly.

The MLA sponsors a diversified program of book publications on scholarly and professional subjects. Books are published singly and in series (write Joseph Hollander, Head of Publications Division, for information). Series include Approaches to Teaching World Literature, Research and Scholarship in Composition, Introductions to Scholarship, Options for Teaching, Technologies and the Humanities, Reviews of Research, Selected Bibliographies in Language and Literature, and Introductions to Older Languages.

Reference works include the *MLA International Bibliography*, available in print, online, and on compact disc, which indexes over 43,000 entries each year and the *Directory of Periodicals*, which provides information on the journals and series the *Bibliography* surveys. Other reference tools range from Wing's *Short-Title Catalogue of Books Printed in England* to the bibliography *Asian American Literature* and from the *MLA Handbook for Writers of Research Papers*, designed for student use, to *Language, Gender, and Professional Writing*. The association's Commission on the Status of Women, Committee on the Literatures and Languages of America, and Committee on the New Variorum Edition of Shakespeare sponsor additional publications as do ADE and ADFL.

The annual convention of the MLA, which in recent years has had an attendance of more than ten thousand, is the largest meeting of its kind in the humanities. Each year there are nearly eight hundred sessions, ranging from small, informal discussions on specialized topics to large forums on subjects of broad general interest. Special events often include poetry readings and film screenings. Over one hundred officially recognized allied organizations of the MLA may also arrange one or two meetings as well as business and social events.

    1990: 27–30 Dec., Chicago, IL
    1991: 27–30 Dec., San Francisco, CA

The MLA issues the *MLA Job Information List* four times a year in English and foreign language editions (both lists include comparative literature, ESL, and linguistics positions). With the cooperation of ADE and ADFL, the MLA sponsors preconvention workshops and the Job Information Center at the annual convention.

Prizes awarded

James Russell Lowell Prize for an outstanding book — a literary or linguistic study, critical edition, or critical biography — by a member

Howard R. Marraro Prize for a distinguished scholarly study by a member on any phase of Italian literature or comparative literature involving Italian

William Riley Parker Prize for an outstanding article in *PMLA*

MLA Prize for Independent Scholars for distinguished research in the modern languages or literatures, including English

Mina P. Shaughnessy Prize for outstanding innovative research in the field of teaching English language and literature

Kenneth W. Mildenberger Prize for outstanding innovative research in the field of teaching foreign languages and literatures

The MLA undertakes periodic surveys of foreign language enrollments and foreign language entrance and degree requirements in United States colleges and universities and of the placement of PhDs in English, foreign languages, comparative literature, and linguistics.

The Foreign Language Programs Office sponsors a series of summer institutes for experienced foreign language professionals with supervisory responsibility from school districts, colleges, and universities.

In association with the Federation of State Humanities Councils and with support from the University of Pittsburgh, the MLA will sponsor a conference on literacy, public policy, and the schools in Pittsburgh, PA, 13–16 September 1990.

The MLA's standing committees sponsor publications, convention programs, and a variety of other activities as charged by the association's Executive Council. The council appoints ad hoc committees to meet particular needs.

The MLA is a member of NHA, the American Council on Education, JNCL, and ACLS.

94.   National Association for Ethnic Studies (NAES)
Department of English
Arizona State University
Tempe, AZ 85287-0302
Founded 1972
Editor of Publications: Gretchen M. Bataille
The association promotes activities and scholarship in the field of ethnic studies.

Periodicals

Explorations in Ethnic Studies. Semiannual. Interdisciplinary journal devoted to the study of ethnicity, ethnic groups, intergroup relations, and the cultural life of ethnic minorities.

Explorations in Sights and Sounds. Annual review of books and nonprint media of interest to teachers, students, librarians, and scholars of ethnic studies as well as community organizations.

The Ethnic Reporter. Semiannual newsletter.

The annual conference assembles a committed group of people to evaluate their own history, to assess the present status of ethnicity, and to examine possibilities for identity and ethnic inclusion. Additional regional meetings offer a forum for the discussion of issues relevant to local communities.

1990: 8-11 Mar., Ft. Collins, CO; Ethnicity, Justice, and the National Experience

1991: 7-10 Mar., Tempe, AZ; Ethnic Studies for the Twentieth-Century

1992: 5-8 Mar., Boca Raton, FL; Ethnicity and Racism in the Americas

The Ernest M. Pon Award is made each year to a community organization working with Asian populations.

The Executive Council of twelve members includes scholars and professionals who are available as consultants to ethnic studies programs.

95. National Association for Foreign Student Affairs (NAFSA)

1860 19th Street, NW
Washington, DC 20009
Founded 1948
6,000 members
Tel. 202 462-4811
Executive Vice President: John F. Reichard

NAFSA provides training, information, and other educational services to professionals in the field of international exchange. NAFSA's members — from every state and over fifty other countries — represent academic institutions, organizations, and individuals concerned with the advancement of effective international education exchange. Five professional sections reflect the interests of members: Admissions Section, Administrators and Teachers in English as a Second Language (see ATESL), Council of Advisers to Foreign Students and Scholars, Community Section, and Section of US Students Abroad.

Periodicals

NAFSA Newsletter. Ed. Richard Getrich. Pub. 8 times a year.
Government Affairs Bulletin. Ed. William Carroll. Pub. 8 times a year.

NAFSA publishes on a wide range of topics related to international exchange. Recent titles have included *Admission and Placement of Students from Central America*; *Crisis Management in a Cross-Cultural Setting*; *Culture, Learning and the Disciplines: Theory and Practice in Cross-Cultural Orientation*; and the videotape *Education for International Development: Professional Integration for a Smooth Passage Home.* Federal grants and NAFSA's general fund make it possible for NAFSA to publish short bibliographies and pamphlets, charging only for postage and handling; titles range from *Academic Advising of Graduate Students from Developing Nations* to *The Risks and Realities of Health Insurance.*

NAFSA convenes its members annually on national and on twelve regional levels to examine critical issues facing the international education field. Approximately ten percent of the attendees at the national conference are from countries other than the United States. Each year NAFSA awards over one hundred travel grants to allow newcomers to attend regional conferences and workshops related to international educational exchange.

1990: 15–18 May, Portland, OR
1991: 24–27 May, Boston, MA
1992: 23–26 May, Chicago, IL

The Job Registry, open to all members, reports on job openings monthly or more frequently, keeps résumés on file, and confers with members at the annual convention.

NAFSA awards cooperative grants in support of campus and community programs and activities that enrich the experience of foreign students living in the United States, enhance the preparation and return of American students studying abroad, and improve and expand the competencies of those who work in international education.

NAFSA currently participates in annual or biannual professional exchanges for international educators with the People's Republic of China and the Baden-Wuerttemberg Ministerium für Wissenschaft und Kunst, Federal Republic of Germany. As one of five members of the National Liaison Committee on Foreign Student Admissions (NLC), NAFSA assists in conducting overseas workshops, evaluating foreign educational credentials, and gathering and sharing on request information on foreign student recruiters.

NAFSA consultants visit postsecondary institutions and community groups to help strengthen their foreign student and scholar services, ESL programs, foreign student admissions, community programs, services for students abroad, and international programs in the overall institutional context. NAFSA's field service annually sponsors dozens of regional workshops, approximately six national seminars, and the Wyoming NAFSA Summer Institute on Foreign Teaching Assistants.

NAFSA provides a voice on regulatory and legislative matters through direct communication with government agencies and participates with other educational associations in activities of major importance to the international educational field. NAFSA is a founding member of the International Educational Exchange Liaison Group, which communicates with members of Congress and other United States government personnel on legislation, federal regulations, and national policy; NAFSA is also a founding member of JNCL.

96.   National Association of Professors of Hebrew (NAPH)

1346 Van Hise Hall
University of Wisconsin
Madison, WI 53406
Founded 1962
400 members
Tel. 608 262-2968
Vice President: Gilead Morahg

NAPH advances the cause of research, scholarship, and university teaching in areas related to Hebrew language, Hebrew literature, and the Bible and provides service and information to teachers of Hebrew in institutions of higher learning.

Periodicals
Hebrew Studies. Ed. Michael V. Fox. Annual. Research and scholarship in Hebrew language and literature.
Bulletin of Higher Hebrew Education. Ed. Rina Donchin. Annual. Methodology and pedagogy of university teaching of modern and biblical Hebrew.
Iggeret. Ed. Zev Garber. Semiannual newsletter. Notes on meetings, members, recent publications, fellowships, grants, and job openings.

Meetings
    1990: May, New York, NY
    1991: May, Berkeley, CA
NAPH also holds an annual autumn session for the presentation of papers and deliberations in conjunction with the national convention of the Society for Biblical Literature and the American Academy of Religion (see SBL and AAR).

97.   National Council of Teachers of English (NCTE)
    1111 Kenyon Road
    Urbana, IL 61801
Founded 1911
58,000 individuals; 57,000 institutions
Tel. 217 328-3870
Executive Director: John C. Maxwell
The aim of NCTE, an association of teachers of English at all levels of education, is to improve the teaching of English. There are three constituent groups of the NCTE: the Conference on College Composition and Communication (CCCC), the Conference on English Education (CEE), and the Conference for Secondary School English Department Chairpersons (CSSEDC).

Periodicals
Language Arts. Ed. David Dillon (McGill Univ.). Pub. 8 times a year. For elementary teachers and teacher trainers.
English Journal. Ed. Ben F. Nelms (Univ. of Missouri, Columbia). Pub. 8 times a year. For junior and senior high school and middle school teachers.
College English. Ed. James Raymond (Univ. of Alabama). Pub. 8 times a year. A professional journal for the college teacher-scholar.
College Composition and Communication. Ed. Richard Gebhardt (Bowling Green Univ.). CCCC's quarterly for teachers of writing in two- and four-year colleges.
English Education. Ed. Mary K. Healy (Univ. of California, Berkeley) and Gordon M. Pradl (New York Univ.). CEE's quarterly for instructors involved in teacher preparation and in-service education.
CSSEDC Quarterly. Ed. James Strickland (Slippery Rock Univ.). For chairs of English departments in secondary schools.
Research in the Teaching of English. Ed. Arthur N. Applebee and Judith Langer (State Univ. of New York, Albany). Quarterly. Interdisciplinary research related to the intersections among schooling, language, and learning at all levels.
Teaching English in the Two-Year College. Ed. Nell Ann Pickett (Hinds Junior Coll.). Quarterly. For teachers of composition, basic writing, grammar, and business and technical writing.

The SLATE Newsletter. Pub. 3 times a year. Summarizes national news that affects language arts educators.

Quarterly Review of Doublespeak. Ed. William Lutz (Rutgers Univ.). Analysis of ambiguous language.

NCTE publishes books, pamphlets, and reference aids on both professional matters and the teaching of writing, language, literature, and nonprint media. It also makes available cassette recordings of speeches on professional issues and videotapes for in-service and teacher training. Books published in 1988 include the following:

> *Rehearsing the Audience: Ways to Develop Student Perceptions about Theatre.* By Ken Davis.
>
> *Focus on Collaborative Learning: Classroom Practices in Teaching English, 1988.* By Jeff Golub and the NCTE Committee on Classroom Practices.
>
> *Unlocking Shakespeare's Language: Help for the Teacher and Student.* By Randall Robinson.
>
> *Talking into Writing: Exercises for Basic Writers.* By Donald L. Rubin and William M. Dodd.
>
> *Teaching Poetry Writing to Adolescents.* By Joseph I. Tsujimoto.

NCTE's annual convention in November, the convention of CCCC, and the spring conference on elementary and secondary English education rotate on a four-year cycle that takes them to each geographical region of the United States in turn.

> Annual convention
> > 1990: 16–21 Nov., Atlanta, GA
> > 1991: 22–27 Nov., Seattle, WA
>
> Spring conference
> > 1990: 7–10 Mar., Colorado Springs, CO
> > 1991: 14–16 Mar., Indianapolis, IN
>
> CCCC
> > 1990: 21–24 Mar., Chicago, IL
> > 1991: 20–23 Mar., Boston, MA

Programs to encourage students in their writing include Achievement Awards in Writing, for high school students (maximum of 876 awards possible); Promising Young Writers, for eighth-grade students (441 awards); and the Program to Recognize Excellence in Student Literary Magazines, in senior high, junior high, and middle schools.

Five types of grants are available through the NCTE Research Foundation: regular grants, awarded to professional researchers, including graduate students conducting dissertation research; teacher-researcher grants, awarded to preK–14 teachers for classroom-based research on the teaching of English and language arts; collaboration grants, intended to foster collaborative research conducted by preK–14 classroom teachers and university researchers; special project grants, available to official NCTE subgroups; and challenge grants, available to local, state, and regional affiliates of NCTE.

NCTE serves its members through a network of more than 130 local, state, and regional affiliate councils; three section committees — elementary, secondary, and college; special interest groups such as the Assembly on Literature for Adolescents and the International Assembly; and committees and commissions concentrating on the major concerns of the profession.

NCTE is an allied organization of the MLA.

98.   National Women's Studies Association (NWSA)
University of Maryland
College Park, MD 20742-1325
Founded 1977
4,000 members
Tel. 301 454-3757
National Director: Caryn McTighe Musil
NWSA promotes feminist education through classroom teaching, research, public policy, and community-based women's advocacy groups. Through women's studies, NWSA seeks to influence the public's perception of women's lives.

Periodicals
NWSA Journal. Ed. Mary Jo Wagner. Quarterly. Features scholarly articles that link teaching to activism.
NWSAction. Ed. Ruby Sales. Quarterly newsletter.
The Women's Studies Program Directory. Biannual.
A Guide to Graduate Work in Women's Studies. Biannual.

The twelfth annual meeting, Feminist Education: Calling the Question, will take place 20–24 June 1990 at the University of Akron, Akron, OH.

NWSA awards $1,000 for the best manuscript in women's studies, which is then published by the University of Illinois Press; a $1,000 graduate scholarship in lesbian studies, and a $1,000 and a $500 graduate scholarship in women's studies; a $500 award in Jewish women's studies; and a $500 fellowship to a Chinese woman from the Republic of China.

The national director does consulting with women's studies programs.

NWSA sells audio- and videotapes for classroom use.

99.   Northeast American Society for Eighteenth-Century Studies (NEASECS)
Department of English
University of Rhode Island
Kingston, RI 02881
Founded 1977
350 members
Tel. 401 789-7131
Secretary-Treasurer: Edna Steeves
NEASECS, a regional affiliate of ASECS, promotes research and scholarship in the area of eighteenth-century studies. It covers the regions of New England and Eastern Canada and the states of Maryland, New York, New Jersey, and Pennsylvania.

Periodical: *NEASECS Newsletter.* Ed. John H. O'Neill (English Dept., Hamilton Coll., Clinton, NY 13323). Pub. 3 times a year.

Meeting: 1990: 1–4 Nov., Univ. of Massachusetts, Amherst, MA

100. Northeast Modern Language Association (NEMLA)
Box 546
Middlebury, VT 05753
Founded 1968
2,200 members
Tel. 802 545-2474
Executive Director: Ida H. Washington
NEMLA, a regional affiliate of the MLA, was formed to promote study, criticism, and research in English and foreign languages and literatures and to further the common interests of teachers and scholars in these disciplines.

Periodical: *Modern Language Studies.* Ed. David Hirsch and Nelson Vieira (Dept. of English, Box 1852, Brown Univ., Providence, RI 02912). Quarterly.

Meetings
> 1990: 6–8 Apr., Toronto, ON
> 1991: 5–7 Apr., Hartford, CT

NEMLA jointly sponsors with Ohio University Press an annual book prize of $1,000 plus publication for a manuscript in English, and with Peter Lang Publishing an annual book prize of $1,000 plus publication for a manuscript in a foreign language field. NEMLA awards several $1,000 summer study and research fellowships and sponsors a joint fellowship with the American Antiquarian Society.

101. Organization of American Historians (OAH)
112 North Bryan Street
Bloomington, IN 47408
Founded 1907
8,000 individuals; 3,400 institutional members
Tel. 812 855-7311
Acting Executive Secretary: Arnita A. Jones
The organization promotes historical study and research in the field of American history.

Periodicals
Journal of American History. Ed. David Thelen. Quarterly.
OAH Newsletter. Ed. Howard McMains. Quarterly.

OAH publishes classroom materials such as *Documents of the United States Constitutional History*; the curriculum guides *Restoring Women to History: Materials for US History* and *Restoring Women to History: Materials for Western Civilization*; and pamphlets on public history such as *Historic Preservation, Educating Historians for Business, Historical Editing*, and *Teaching Public History to Undergraduates*.

Meetings
> 1990: 22–25 Mar., Washington, DC
> 1991: 11–14 Apr., Louisville, KY
> 1992: 2–5 Apr., Chicago, IL

As part of the annual meeting, OAH presents Focus on Teaching Day, a series of workshops and sessions for middle and high school history teachers.

Prizes awarded
ABC-CLIO America: History and Life Award for scholarship in journal litera-
ture advancing new perspectives on accepted interpretations or previously un-
considered topics
Erik Barnouw Award for outstanding reporting or programming on network or
cable television or in documentary film concerned with American history or
the promotion of history as a lifetime habit
Ray Allen Billington Prize for best book on American frontier history
Binkley-Stephenson Award for best article in the *Journal of American History*
Avery O. Craven Award for most original book on the Civil War years or the
era of reconstruction
Merle Curti Award for books in American social history and intellectual history
Richard W. Leopold Prize for best book written by a historian connected with
federal, state, or municipal government
Louis Pelzer Memorial Award for best unpublished essay in American history
by a graduate student
James A. Rawley Prize for a book about race relations in the United States
Frederick Jackson Turner Award for best book on a significant phase of Ameri-
can history by a previously unpublished author

The Lectureship Program, established in 1981, coordinates and arranges lectures
by prominent scholars on a variety of historical topics.

Service committees of the organization include Committee on Access to Documents and Open Information, Committee on History in the Schools and Colleges, Committee on Teaching, Committee on the Status of Minority Historians
and Minority History, Committee on Public History, and Committee on the Status
of Women in the Historical Profession.

Under the auspices of the National Coordinating Committee for the Promotion
of History, OAH has been represented on a variety of issues of importance to
the historical profession. OAH is a constituent member of ACLS.

102. Pacific Northwest Council of Foreign Languages (PNCFL)
Department of Foreign Languages and Literatures
Oregon State University
Kidder Hall 210
Corvallis, OR 97331-4603
Founded 1950
600 members
Tel. 503 737-2289/2146
Executive Secretary: Ray Verzasconi
PNCFL seeks to improve opportunities for learning foreign languages at all levels
of the educational system. Areas of concern include public awareness, the train-
ing and continuous professional development of teachers, and all the theoretical
and practical issues involved in the teaching of languages, cultures, and literatures.

Periodicals
Selecta: Journal of the PNCFL. Ed. Guy Wood. Annual.
PNCFL Newsletter. Ed. Ray Verzasconi. Quarterly.
HANDS on Language. Ed. Alfred Smith. Annual.

Meetings
    1990: 2–5 May, Portland, OR
    1991: 9–11 May, Spokane, WA

Prizes awarded
Pacific Northwest Teacher of the Year Awards (K–12 and postsecondary), jointly
    sponsored by PNCFL and the National Textbook Company
PNCFL Regional Media Award for support of foreign language studies

PNCFL and the Quebec Government Office, Los Angeles, jointly sponsor two
fellowships annually for teachers of French (grades 7–12) in the PNCFL region.
PNCFL and the Goethe Institute, Seattle, jointly sponsor an annual fellowship
for a teacher of German (grades 7–12) in the PNCFL region.

PNCFL is a member of JNCL and NFMLTA.

103. Philological Association of the Pacific Coast (PAPC)
    Office of Alumni Relations
    Reed College
    Portland, OR 97202
Founded 1899
1,000 members
Tel. 503 777-7589
Executive Directors: Caroline Locher and Ellen Stauder
The object of the association is the advancement and diffusion of philological
knowledge.

Periodicals
Pacific Coast Philology. Annual. Papers selected from the previous year's conference.
Newsletter. Pub. 2 times a year.

PAPC holds an annual fall meeting.

PAPC has been associated since its founding with the APA (American Philological Association) and since 1917 with the MLA.

104. Philosophy of Education Society (PES)
    4080 Villa Vista
    Palo Alto, CA 94306
Founded 1941
500 members
Tel. 415 494-2315
Secretary-Treasurer: Michael S. Katz
The purposes of the society are to promote the fundamental philosophic treatment of the problems of education and the clarification of agreements and differ-
ences among the several philosophies of education through discussion at annual
meetings; to improve teaching in the philosophy of education in schools for the
education of teachers and in other educational institutions; to cultivate fruitful
relations between workers in general philosophy and workers in the philosophy
of education and between scholars of the philosophy of education and those in

other areas of education; and to encourage promising students in the field. Membership is by election only.

Periodicals

Philosophy of Education: Proceedings of the Philosophy of Education Society. Ed. Thomas W. Nelson (Illinois State Univ.). Annual.

Educational Theory. Ed. Ralph C. Page (Univ. of Illinois). Quarterly.

Meeting: 1990: 30 Mar.–2 Apr., Miami, FL

105. Poetry Society of America (PSA)

15 Gramercy Park
New York, NY 10003
Founded 1910
1,700 members
Tel. 212 254-9628
Administrative Director: Elise Paschen

Founded by Witter Bynner, George Santayana, Jessie Rittenhouse, and Edward Wheeler, PSA, the oldest poetry organization in America, is a cultural organization whose mission is to secure a wider recognition for poetry as an important force in cultural life, to kindle a more intelligent appreciation of poetry, and to assist poets, especially younger American poets.

Periodical: *PSA Newsletter.* Pub. 3 times a year. Offers book reviews, interviews with poets, discounts on books, and information pertinent to the art—news of members, notices of new books, and details of deadlines, conferences, and grants.

The society's extensive awards program, now exceeding $14,000 in annual prizes, advances excellence in poetry and encourages skills in traditional forms as well as experiments in contemporary forms. It is also designed to call the attention of the public and the literary world to poets and poetry.

PSA offers readings, lectures, and symposia open to the public at both the New York City headquarters and at regional centers around the country. PSA programs feature beginning writers in the New Poets Reading Series as well as established writers working in all traditions. Workshops led by professional poets in New York provide poets of all levels the opportunity to work with master teachers. The Peer Group Workshop carries on the tradition, begun at the society's founding, of members gathering to share their latest work in an informal group that offers both criticism and appreciation.

The society's Van Voorhis Library, housing over eight thousand volumes of poetry, criticism, biography, and reference, holds a collection of rare volumes of early twentieth-century authors.

106. Popular Culture Association (PCA)

Bowling Green State University
Bowling Green, OH 43403
Founded 1970
3,200 members
Tel. 419 372-2981
Secretary-Treasurer: Ray B. Browne

PCA seeks to broaden and deepen the study of humanities and social sciences, to demonstrate how closely they should be related in education, to develop the reasoning ability of students, and to encourage literacy by beginning study with the familiar and working toward the unfamiliar.

Periodical: *Journal of Popular Culture.* Ed. Ray B. Browne. Quarterly.

In addition to its yearly meeting, PCA's eight regional sections convene annually.
    1990: 8–10 Mar., Toronto, ON
    1991: San Antonio, TX

PCA awards prizes for outstanding work in various fields.

PCA is an allied organization of the MLA.

107. Radical Caucus in English and the Modern Languages
    PO Box 102
    Kendall Square Post Office
    Cambridge, MA 02142
Founded 1968
250-300 members
Tel. 212 570-0997
Secretary: Paul Lauter
The Radical Caucus provides a forum for discussion of the implications of socialist ideas in teaching and educational institutions and of ways to put such ideas into practice. Teachers of English and modern languages and literatures at all levels, including primary and secondary schools, make up the membership.

Periodical: *Radical Teacher.* Pub. 3 times a year. A socialist and feminist journal containing articles on the theory and practice of teaching.

Annual meetings are held in conjunction with the MLA convention.

108. Renaissance English Text Society (RETS)
    Arthur F. Kinney
    Department of English
    University of Massachusetts
    Amherst, MA 01003
Founded 1968
173 members
Tel. 413 545-0372/2332 or 413 256-8648 (home)
President: Arthur F. Kinney
The society publishes rare texts of Renaissance prose and poetry and, at annual meetings, discusses issues of textual editing in old-spelling texts.

Recent book publications include Francis Quarles's *Argalus and Parthenia*, edited by David Freeman; *Cicero's Officiis* in the Nicholas Grimald translation, edited by Gerald O'Gorman; and Thomas Moffet's *Silkwormes and Their Flies*, edited by Victor Houliston. In preparation are John Bale's *Vocacyon* and related documents, edited by Peter Happé and John King; Heliodorus in the Thomas Underdowne translation; the prose works of John Ford; and Lady Mary Wroth's *Urania*.

RETS holds an annual forum at the MLA convention. Thomas Berger (St. Lawrence Univ.) chaired the 1989 forum on old-spelling texts and new critical methods; Josephine Roberts (Louisiana State Univ., Baton Rouge) will chair the 1990 forum on editing letters, diaries, and speeches in Renaissance England.

RETS holds occasional public lectures.

109. Rocky Mountain Modern Language Association (RMMLA)
Department of English
Boise State University
Boise, ID 83725
Founded 1947
1,150 members
Tel. 208 385-1199
Executive Director: Charles G. Davis
The association unites professionals who have allied interests but are spread over a vast geographic area. RMMLA seeks to stimulate consideration, evaluation, and cultivation of languages and literatures by presenting papers at its annual meeting, by discussing problems in the teaching profession, by cooperating with other academic and cultural societies to enrich and strengthen cultural life in the Rocky Mountain States, and by publishing a regular bulletin.

Periodical: *Rocky Mountain Review of Language and Literature*. Ed. Carol A. Martin (Dept. of English, Boise State Univ., Boise, ID 83725). Quarterly. Scholarly articles, essays on the teaching of languages and literatures, fiction, poetry, and reviews.

Meeting: 1990: 11–13 Oct., Salt Lake City, UT

The association sponsors the RMMLA-Huntington Award, a stipend of $1,500 to scholars who wish to work for one month at the Huntington Library.

RMMLA is a regional affiliate of MLA.

110. Science Fiction Research Association (SFRA)
855 South Harvard Drive
Palatine, IL 60097
Founded 1970
350 members
Tel. 312 991-6009
President: Elizabeth Anne Hull
SFRA, the oldest professional organization for the study of science fiction, fantasy, and utopias, promotes scholarly interest in these areas and provides a forum for the interchange of information and interpretation. SFRA seeks to improve classroom teaching, encourage and assist scholarship, and evaluate and publicize new books and magazines on fantastic literature and film.

Periodicals
Extrapolation. Ed. Donald Hassler (Kent State Univ., Kent, OH). Quarterly. Critical, historical, and bibliographic articles and reviews.
Science-Fiction Studies. Ed. Robert Philmus (Concordia Univ., Montreal, PQ). Pub. 3 times a year.

SFRA Newsletter. Pub. 10 times a year. News, reviews, short criticism, interviews, and work-in-progress reports.
SFRA Directory. Ed. David G. Mead. Annual.

Meetings
      1990: 28 June–1 July, Long Beach, CA
      1991: late June, Iowa City, IA

SFRA sponsors the annual Pilgrim Award for lifetime contribution to scholarship and criticism in science fiction and fantasy and the SFRA Award for scholarship.

111. Société Rencesvals, American-Canadian Branch
      Department of French
      University of Virginia
      Charlottesville, VA 22903
Founded 1955
96 members
Tel. 804 924-7157
Secretary-Treasurer: Robert Francis Cook
The society aims to coordinate activity of the American and Canadian members of the Société Internationale Rencesvals and to promote the study of medieval epic literature in the various Romance tongues.

Periodicals
Bulletin Bibliographique de la Société Rencesvals. Annual.
Olifant. Quarterly. Ed. William W. Kibler (Dept. of French and Italian, Univ. of Texas, Austin, TX 78712-1197). Articles on Medieval epic literature in the Romance languages and epic in general.

The American-Canadian Branch meets twice each year, at the MLA convention in December and at the International Medieval Conference in May. Problems in the Romance Epic was the topic at the 1989 MLA convention. Every three years the society holds its International Congress; the next congress is planned for 6–12 August 1991 in Edinburgh, Scotland.

112. Society for Critical Exchange (SCE)
      Department of English
      Miami University
      Oxford, OH 45056
Founded 1976
200 members
Tel. 513 529-5263 or 523-8574
Executive Director: James T. Sosnoski
SCE encourages cooperative inquiry and research in criticism and theory. The society is designed to develop through exchanges among its members.

Periodicals
Critical Exchange. Pub. 2 times a year. A journal of research in progress.

SCE News and Notices. News of recent and upcoming events, updates on SCE projects, and announcements of general interest to the membership.
Occasional monographs.

In addition to sponsoring sessions at the MLA convention and regional meetings, SCE holds an annual meeting. The topic of the 1989 meeting, held at Miami University, Oxford, OH, was Alternative Perspectives for Critical Theory: The Works of Barbara Herrnstein Smith.

SCE currently sponsors three major collaborative research projects organized and coordinated by its members: the GRIP project (Group for Research on the Institutionalization and Professionalization of Literary Study), directed by David Shumway (Carnegie Melon Univ.); the PRISM project, directed by Patricia Harkin (Univ. of Akron), an investigation of the interrelations among writing, reading, rhetoric, and literary theory; and Feminism and Its Discontents, organized by Dale Bauer and Kristina Straub (Miami Univ.), an examination of feminist political strategies in the academy.

113. Society for Ethnomusicology (SEM)
Morrison Hall 005
Indiana University
Bloomington, IN 47405-2501
Founded 1953
2,500 members
Tel. 812 855-6672
Secretary: Joseph Hickerson
SEM's object is the advancement of research and study in the field of ethnomusicology; all interested persons, regardless of race, creed, color, or national origin, are encouraged to become members. SEM aims to serve the membership and society at large through the dissemination of knowledge concerning the music of the world's peoples.

Periodicals
Ethnomusicology: Journal of the Society of Ethnomusicology. Ed. Charles Capwell. Pub. 3 times a year.
SEM Newsletter. Ed. Laurel Sercombe and Chris Waterman. Pub. 3 times a year.

Publications
A Discography of the Art Music of India. By Elise B. Barnett. 1974.
Recordings of the Traditional Music of Bali and Lombok. By Andrew Toth. 1980.
Tutelo Rituals on Six Nations Reserve, Ontario. By Gertrude Prodosch Kurath. 1981.
Women in North American Indian Music. Ed. Richard Keeling. 1989.

Meeting: 1990: 7–10 Nov., Oakland, CA

Prizes awarded
Jaap Kunst Prize for best student paper published in *Ethnomusicology*
Charles Seeger Prize for most distinguished paper read by a student at the annual meeting
Klaus Wachsmann Prize for best published work on organology

SEM is a constituent member of ACLS.

114. **Society for German Renaissance and Baroque Literature (SGRABL)**
S-326 Burrowes
Pennsylvania State University
University Park, PA 16802
Founded 1982
87 members
Tel. 814 865-5481
National Treasurer: Barton W. Browning
The society promotes the study and exchange of ideas about German Renaissance and baroque literature.

The society maintains informal relations with the quarterly *Daphnis: Zeitschrift für Mittlere Deutsche Literatur,* edited by Hans-Gert Roloff.

The annual meeting is held at the MLA convention.

115. **Society for the Advancement of Scandinavian Study (SASS)**
Department of Germanic Languages and Literatures
University of Oregon
Eugene, OR 97403
Founded 1911
Tel. 503 346-6405
Secretary-Treasurer: Virpi Zuck
SASS is an association of scholars and others interested in the cultures of the Nordic Countries: Denmark, Finland, Iceland, Norway, and Sweden. The society promotes Scandinavian study and instruction in the Unites States; encourages original research in the fields of Scandinavian languages, literatures, history, culture, and society, and provides a medium for the publication of the results of such research; and fosters closer relations among persons interested in Scandinavian studies in the United States and elsewhere.

Periodical: *Scandinavian Studies.* Ed. by Faith Ingwersen and Niels Ingwersen (Univ. of Wisconsin, Madison). Quarterly. Topics covered include philological and linguistic problems of the Scandinavian languages, medieval and modern; the literatures of Denmark, the Faeroes, Finland (Finno-Swedish and Finnish), Iceland, Norway, and Sweden; and the history, society, and culture of the North.

Meeting: 1990: 3–5 May, Madison, WI

116. **Society for the History of Technology (SHOT)**
Department of History
Duke University
Durham, NC 27706
Founded 1958
1,500 members
Tel. 919 684-2758
Secretary: Alex Roland
The society encourages the study of the development of technology and its relation to society and culture.

Periodicals
Technology and Culture. Ed. Robert Post. Quarterly.
SHOT Newsletter. Ed. Alex Roland. Quarterly.

Meetings
      1990: Oct., Cleveland, OH
      1991: Oct., Madison, WI

The society sponsors or administers seven prizes, all designed to encourage and recognize distinguished contributions to scholarship or museum exhibitry in the history of technology:
Leonardo da Vinci Medal, the society's highest award, for an outstanding contribution to the history of technology by an individual
Dexter Prize for the best book in the field
Abbott Payson Usher Prize for the best article published by SHOT
Joan Cahalin Robinson Prize for the best paper presented at the annual meeting by a young scholar
Samuel Eleazer and Rose Tartakow Levinson Prize for an original essay that is the author's first work in the field
IEEE (Institute of Electrical and Electronics Engineers) Life Members' Prize in Electrical History for the best article in electrical history
Dibner Prize for excellence in museum exhibits that interpret for the general public the history of technology, industry, and engineering

SHOT is a constituent member of ACLS.

117. Society for the Study of Midwestern Literature (SSML)
      229 Bessey Hall
      Michigan State University
      East Lansing, MI 48823-1033
Founded 1976
300 members
Tel. 517 353-4370
Executive Secretary: David D. Anderson
The society fosters scholarship on midwestern literature.

Periodicals
Mid-America. Ed. David D. Anderson. Annual.
Midwestern Miscellany. Ed. David D. Anderson. Annual.
SSML Newsletter. Ed. David D. Anderson. Pub. 3 times a year.

SSML conducts an annual symposium each spring on the cultural heritage of the Midwest and the concurrent Midwestern Poetry Festival. The 1990 conference will be held in East Lansing, MI, in mid-May.

Best Paper and Best Poem Awards of $250 each are underwritten by a gift from Gwendolyn Brooks.

118. Society for the Study of Multi-Ethnic Literature of the United States (MELUS)
2-C Buckboard Lane
Greensboro, NC 27410
Founded 1973
390 members
Tel. 919 852-6591 or 334-7764
President: SallyAnn H. Ferguson

MELUS endeavors to expand the definition of American literature through the study and teaching of Afro-American, American Indian, Asian and Pacific American, Hispanic, and ethnically specific European American literary works, their authors, and their cultural contexts.

Periodicals

MELUS. Ed. Joseph T. Skerrett, Jr. (272 Bartlett Hall, Univ. of Massachusetts, Amherst, MA 01003). Quarterly.

MELUS NewsNotes. Ed. Shirley Lumpkin (Dept. of English, Marshall Univ., Huntington, WV). Pub. 4–6 times a year.

MELUS Directory. Pub. every 3 years.

The society meets twice a year, at the MLA convention and at the National MELUS Conference. The theme of the 1990 conference, to be held in Chicago, 20–21 April, is Migrations and Immigrations in Ethnic American Literature.

MELUS presents an annual award for distinguished work in the study of ethnic literature.

119. Society for the Study of Narrative Literature (SSNL)
Eastern Michigan University
Ypsilanti, MI 48197
Founded 1984
425 members
Tel. 313 971-1893
Secretary-Treasurer: Barbara Perkins

The society brings together scholars from different fields and different critical orientations with a common interest in narrative theory and literature.

Periodical: *The Journal of Narrative Technique.* Ed. George Perkins and Barbara Perkins. Pub. 3 times a year.

Publication: *Narrative Poetics: Innovations, Limits, Challenges.* Ed. James Phelan. Columbus: Ohio State UP, 1987.

The 1990 International Conference on Narrative Theory will be held in New Orleans, LA, 4–7 April, under the sponsorship of Tulane University and SSNL.

120. Society for the Study of Southern Literature (SSSL)
Box 2625
Mississippi State University
Mississippi State, MS 39762

Founded 1968
375 members
Tel. 601 325-2408/3644
Secretary-Treasurer: Susan Snell
The society promotes the study of southern literature, history, and culture. Members include scholars, librarians, and others in these and related fields.

The *Newsletter of the Society for the Study of Southern Literature*, edited by Susan Snell, appears twice a year. "A Checklist of Scholarship in Southern Literature," compiled by the Committee on Bibliography, appears annually in the Spring issue of the *Mississippi Quarterly*.

SSSL has sponsored or helped to publish several scholarly studies of Southern literature. The most recent title is *The History of Southern Literature*, edited by Louis D. Rubin (Baton Rouge: Louisiana State UP, 1985).

The society meets formally at the MLA convention and informally at SAMLA and SCMLA conferences.

The society awards the C. Hugh Holman Award for literary scholarship.

The society sponsors the Discussion Group on Southern Literature in conjunction with the MLA.

121. Society for Utopian Studies (SUS)
Department of Political Science
University of Missouri-St. Louis
St. Louis, MO 63121-4499
Founded 1973
200 members
Tel. 314 553-5849
Chair, Steering Committee: Lyman Tower Sargent
SUS is an international, interdisciplinary association devoted to the study of both literary and experimental utopias. Scholars in the association approach utopian studies from such diverse backgrounds as classics, economics, engineering, history, literature, philosophy, political science, psychology, sociology, foreign languages, and the arts, and among the members are architects, futurists, urban planners, and environmentalists. Membership is open to all persons with utopian interests.

Periodicals
Utopus Discovered. Ed. Carol A. Kolmerten. Pub. 2-3 times a year. Newsletter.
Utopian Studies. Ed. Lyman Tower Sargent. Semiannual.
Directory of Utopian Scholars. Ed. Arthur O. Lewis. Annual.

Meetings
1990: 15-18 Nov., Louisville, KY
1991: Nov., Las Vegas, NV

The Arthur O. Lewis Award honors the best paper presented by a young scholar at the annual meeting.

122. Society of Architectural Historians (SAH)
1232 Pine Street
Philadelphia, PA 19107
Founded 1940
3,500 members
Tel. 215 735-0224
Executive Director: David Bahlman

The society provides an international forum for persons interested in architecture and the related arts. It encourages scholarly research in the field and promotes the preservation of significant architectural monuments that are an integral part of our worldwide historical and cultural heritage. The work of the society is significant for architects, planners, teachers, scholars, libraries, historical societies, museums, students, and all those who care about architecture and the protection of buildings of historic and aesthetic importance.

Periodicals
The Journal of the Society of Architectural Historians. Quarterly.
Newsletter. Pub. 6 times a year. Includes placement information and the Forum of the Committee on Preservation.

Each spring meeting lasting four to six days is held in a city of significant architectural interest. The program includes the presentation of papers, architectural tours of the area, and relevant exhibitions and receptions.
1990: 28 Mar.–1 Apr., Boston, MA

Prizes awarded
Alice Davis Hitchcock Award for the most distinguished work of scholarship by a North American scholar
Founders' Award for the best *Journal* article by a young scholar
Antoinette Forrester Downing Award for excellence in published architectural surveys

The society awards a Domestic Tour Scholarship to allow a graduate student to attend the year's domestic tour and the Rosann Berry Fellowship for a graduate student to attend the annual meeting.

At least one foreign and one American or Canadian architectural study tour, and often more, normally led by authorities on the area, are held every year in regions of special architectural interest.

SAH has twenty-four state and regional chapters and two special-interest chapters: Decorative Arts and Census of Stained Glass Windows in America. The society is a constituent member of ACLS and is affiliated with the Society of Architectural Historians, Great Britain.

123. Society of Biblical Literature (SBL)
819 Houston Mill Road, NE
Atlanta, GA 30329
Founded 1880
5,250 members
Tel. 404 636-4744
Executive Director: David J. Lull

SBL's purpose is to stimulate the critical investigation of classical biblical literatures, together with related literatures, by the exchange of scholarly research both in published form and in a public forum. The society supports those disciplines and subdisciplines pertinent to the illumination of the literatures and religions of the ancient Near East and Mediterranean regions, such as the study of ancient languages, textual criticism, history, and archaeology.

Journal of Biblical Literature, edited by John J. Collins (Univ. of Notre Dame), examines the canon, the cognate literature, and the historical matrix of the Bible from a technical perspective. Experimental in both form and content, *Semeia*, edited by Robert C. Culley (McGill Univ.), employs the methods, models, and findings of linguistics, folklore studies, contemporary literary criticism, structuralism, social anthropology, and other such disciplines to open new areas in biblical studies. Both are published quarterly. SBL also publishes the following periodicals in association with the American Academy of Religion (see AAR):

Religious Studies News. Pub. 5 times a year.

Critical Review of Books in Religion. Ed. by Beverly Roberts Gaventa (Columbia Theological Sem.). Annual.

Openings. Bimonthly placement assistance service.

The Scholars Press publishes books sponsored by SBL. Recent titles include the following:

Greco-Roman Literature and the New Testament: Selected Forms and Genres. Ed. David E. Aune.

In an Age of Prose: A Literary Approach to Ezra-Nehemiah. By Tamara C. Eskenazi.

Signs and Wonders: Biblical Texts in Literary Focus. Ed. J. Cheryl Exum.

Fragments from Hellenistic Jewish Authors. Vol. 2. By Carl R. Holladay.

The Pre-Biblical Narrative Tradition. By Simon B. Parker.

Meetings

    1990: 17–20 Nov., New Orleans, LA

    1991: 23–26 Nov., Kansas City, MO

SBL convenes jointly with AAR. Twelve regional SBL meetings are held each year in early spring.

SBL is a constituent member of ACLS.

124. South Asian Literary Association (SALA)

    Department of Language and Literature

    University of North Florida

    4567 St. John's Bluff Road South

    Jacksonville, FL 32216

Founded 1974

120 members

Tel. 904 646-2818

Secretary-Treasurer: Satya S. Pachori

SALA seeks to generate and foster scholarship in the languages and literatures of India, Nepal, Pakistan, Sri Lanka, Bangladesh, and other countries of the South Asia region. Members include students, professors, and nonacademics interested in South Asian studies, comparative literature, and East-West literary relations.

Periodicals
South Asian Review. Ed. Satya S. Pachori. Annual. Articles on South Asian literatures and languages and comparative studies of East-West literary relations
as well as special issues on major authors, movements, and themes.
SALA Newsletter. Pub. 2 times a year.

SALA sponsors at least two scholarly sessions and one business meeting during
every annual convention of the MLA.

SALA is an allied organization of the MLA.

125. South Atlantic Modern Language Association (SAMLA)
CB 3530, 120 Dey Hall
University of North Carolina
Chapel Hill, NC 27599-3530
Founded 1928
4,500 members
Tel. 919 962-7165
Executive Director: Siegfried Mews
SAMLA's objectives are the advancement of scholarship and teaching in the modern
languages and literatures in the states of Alabama, Florida, Georgia, Kentucky,
Maryland, North Carolina, South Carolina, Tennessee, Virginia, West Virginia,
and in the District of Columbia.

Periodicals
South Atlantic Review. Ed. Siegfried Mews. Quarterly.
SAMLA News. Annual.

Meetings
1990: 15–17 Nov., Tampa, FL
1991: 14–16 Nov., Atlanta, GA
Job placement services are available at the annual convention.

Prizes awarded
SAMLA Studies Award for an unpublished manuscript
Prize for best article in the *SAR*

SAMLA is a regional affiliate of the MLA.

126. South Central Modern Language Association (SCMLA)
Department of English
Texas A&M University
College Station, TX 77843-4238
Founded 1940
1,600 members
Tel. 409 845-7041
Executive Director: Richard Critchfield
The primary purpose of SCMLA is the advancement of scholarship, teaching,
and research in the modern languages and literatures in the states of Texas, Loui-
siana, Tennessee, Oklahoma, Arkansas, and Mississippi.

Periodicals
South Central Review. Ed. Kenneth M. Price. Quarterly.
South Central Newsletter. Ed. Richard Critchfield. Semiannual.

Since the 1988 convention at Arlington, TX, when Carlos Fuentes spoke on History and Fiction: The Epic of the Conquest of Mexico, SCMLA has invited a renowned writer or poet to speak at each annual meeting. The 1990 meeting will be held 25-27 October in San Antonio, TX.

The Kirby Award is given annually to the author of an outstanding article in the *South Central Review.*

SCMLA currently awards seven research grants: two $500 stipends for research abroad, one $500 grant for a graduate student working on a dissertation, one $500 stipend in the United States at the institution of the applicant's choice, one $1,500 collaborative grant with the Huntington Library, one $1000 collaborative grant with the Humanities Research Center at the Univ. of Texas, Austin, and one $750 collaborative grant with the Newberry Library for one month's residency.

SCMLA is a regional affiliate of the MLA.

127. Southeast American Society for French Seventeenth-Century Studies (SE17)
Department of Romance Languages
University of Georgia
Athens, GA 30602
Founded 1982
250 members
Tel. 404 542-3164; FAX 404 542-3287
Chair, Executive Committee: Francis Assaf
SE17 encourages scholarship in French seventeenth-century studies. Membership is open to anyone with a serious interest in French seventeenth-century studies, as evidenced by teaching, research, or other activities.

Periodical: *Cahiers du Dix-septième.* Ed. Francis Assaf. Semiannual.

SE17 meets the last weekend of September or the first weekend of October each year; topics are decided at the previous year's meeting. In 1990, the society will convene in Columbia, SC.

128. Speech Communication Association (SCA)
5105 Backlick Road, Suite E
Annandale, VA 22003
Founded 1914
6,000 members
Tel. 703 750-0533
Executive Director: James L. Guardino
SCA promotes study, criticism, research, teaching, and application of the artistic, humanistic, and scientific principles of communication, particularly speech communication. With members in every state and over twenty countries, SCA provides forums for professional exchange among scholars, outlets for scholarly papers and books, opportunities for professional service, resources for keeping

abreast of new developments, and a voice for the profession on legislation and other public matters.

Periodicals

The Quarterly Journal of Speech. Includes articles, research reports, and book reviews.

Communication Education. Quarterly.

The Speech Communication Teacher. Quarterly.

Communication Monographs. Quarterly. Devoted mainly to scientific and empirical investigations of communication processes.

Critical Studies in Mass Communication. Quarterly. Focuses exclusively on the range of critical perspectives which help define the expanding area of mass communication research.

Text and Performance Quarterly.

Spectra. Monthly newsletter (no July issue). Includes listings of positions available.

The Speech Communication Directory. Annual.

Free Speech Yearbook. Sponsored by the SCA Commission on Freedom of Speech.

Newsletter. Sponsored by the SCA Commission on Freedom of Speech.

The Directory of Graduate Programs in the Communication Arts and Sciences. Biennial.

Index to Journals in Communication Studies. Pub. every five years.

Publications

Mediation: Toward a Civilized System of Dispute Resolution. By John W. Keltner. 1987.

Interethnic Communication: Current Research. Vol. 10. Ed. Young Yun Kim. 1986.

How Do Teachers Communicate? A Review and Critique of Assessment Practices. Ed. Joseph L. McCaleb. 1987.

In addition to publishing books and pamphlets, SCA makes available tape recordings in which leading teachers, researchers, and practitioners set forth their ideas.

Meetings

    1990: 1–4 Nov., Chicago, IL
    1991: 30 Oct.–3 Nov., Atlanta, GA

SCA also holds an annual summer conference; past topics have included argumentation, the performance of literature, women's communication, and speech communication in community colleges.

The SCA Placement Service maintains confidential files for members and sponsors the Placement Center at the annual convention.

The SCA Research Board and cooperating universities cosponsor Doctoral Honors Seminars, to provide opportunities for PhD candidates to share ideas with their peers and benefit from the critical reactions of established scholars, and Regional Research Seminars, to promote direct interactions among investigators who share research interests and geographical proximity.

SCA is affiliated with the Alliance of Associations for the Advancement of Education, the American Association for the Advancement of Science, the Committee for Education Funding, the National Coalition against Censorship, the National Council on Communicative Disorders, the MLA, and NHA. Eight organizations are affiliated with SCA.

129. Teachers of English to Speakers of Other Languages (TESOL)
Suite 300
1600 Cameron Street
Alexandria, VA 22314
Founded 1966
11,500 members
Tel. 703 836-0774
Executive Director: Richard A. Orem
TESOL seeks to promote scholarship, to distribute information, to strengthen instruction and research at all levels in the teaching of standard English to speakers of other languages or dialects, and to cooperate with other groups having similar concerns.

Periodicals
TESOL Quarterly. Ed. Sandra Silberstein (Dept. of English, Univ. of Washington, Seattle, WA 98195).
TESOL Newsletter. Ed. Jean Zukowski-Faust (Univ. of Northern Arizona).

Publications
Directory of Professional Preparation Programs in TESOL in the United States, 1989–91. Ed. Julia Frank-McNeil. 1989.
A World of Books: An Annotated Reading List for ESL/EFL Students. By Dorothy S. Brown. 1987.
Reviews of English Proficiency Tests. Ed. J. Charles Alderson, Karl J. Krahnke, and Charles W. Stansfield. 1987.
Research in Reading ESL. Ed. Joanne Devine, Patricia L. Carell, and David E. Eskey. 1987.

Meetings
1990: 5–10 Mar., San Francisco, CA
1991: 24–29 Mar., New York, NY
1992: 2–8 Mar., Vancouver, BC

TESOL assists job seekers in the EFL, ESL, and SESD bilingual education fields in four ways: the TESOL Employment Information Service and bimonthly *Bulletin*, the *TESOL Newsletter* Job Openings column, and the Employment Clearinghouse at the TESOL convention. The Field Services Director at TESOL's central office is also available for newcomers entering the field or for more experienced members wishing to enhance their career options.

TESOL offers travel grants as well as awards for research, materials development, service, and teaching to qualified members on a competitive basis.

Consultancy referrals are made on request to assist in developing teacher education, program design and evaluation, and professional standards.

The Professional Standards Committee addresses issues vital to the development of quality ESL and TESOL preparation programs and to the promotion of appropriate employment conditions for TESOL professionals. Standards are fostered through endorsement of the *TESOL Statement of Core Standards for Language and Professional Programs* and a program for institutional self-study.

TESOL's annual summer institute offers courses for undergraduate and graduate students.

The Sociopolitical Concerns Committee acts as a clearinghouse for information on social and political issues and events that effect TESOL members, their students, or their programs.

Members also belong to seventeen interest sections relevant to their professional activities such as elementary education, secondary education, bilingual education, adult education, teacher education, and program administration.

TESOL is a member of JNCL.

130. Twentieth Century Spanish Association of America (TCSAA)
Department of Spanish and Portuguese
University of Colorado
Campus Box 278
Boulder, CO 80309-0278
Founded 1983
600 members
Tel. 303 492-7308
Executive Secretary: Luis T. González-del-Valle
The aim of the association is to expand knowledge of twentieth-century literary studies.

Periodicals
Siglo XX/20th Century. Ed. Luis T. González-del-Valle. Pub. 1-2 times a year.
Anales de la literatura española contemporánea. Ed. Luis T. González-del-Valle. Pub.
    1-3 times a year.

TCSAA meets in association with RMMLA.

Every two years, TCSAA awards the Angle Maria de Lera Hispanism Prize for literature to a distinguished living Spanish or Spanish American writer.

TCSAA sponsors a lecture series throughout the United States.

The association is an affiliate of the Asociación Colegial de Escritores de España.

131. Urban Affairs Association (UAA)
University of Delaware
Newark, DE 19716
Founded 1969
200 members
Tel. 302 451-2394
Executive Director: Mary Helen Callahan
As the international professional association for urbanists, UAA encourages the dissemination of information and research findings about urbanism and urbanization; supports the development of university education, research, and service programs in urban affairs; and provides leadership in fostering urban affairs as a professional and academic field.

Periodicals
Journal of Urban Affairs. Ed. Scott Cumming and Theodore Koebel. Quarterly.
UAA Communication. Newsletter. Includes job information.
Urban Affairs Programs. Regularly updated directory of university programs.

UAA holds an annual meeting each spring; conference programs feature topics related to both institutional concerns and urban issues.
    1990: 18–21 Apr., Charlotte, NC
    1991: 17–20 Apr., Vancouver, BC

Prizes are awarded for the best paper and the best student paper given at the meeting.

Through its secretariat, UAA provides a clearinghouse of information and materials on urban affairs programs; technical advice on organizational and program development; surveys on topics such as the organization and staffing of centers, enrollment, and student placement; and liaisons with other professional and educational organizations.

132. Women in German (WIG)
Department of German
Herter Hall
University of Massachusetts
Amherst, MA 01003
Founded 1976
530 members
Tel. 413 545-0542/0310
Editor of Newsletter: Susan L. Cocalis
WIG facilitates communication among members of the profession interested in feminist scholarship or pedagogy at the secondary and postsecondary level.

Periodicals
WIG Newsletter. Pub. 3 times a year.
Women in German Yearbook.

WIG meets annually each October. The 1990 convention will be held in Minneapolis, MN. WIG also routinely sponsors special sessions at MLA, AATG, and regional MLA meetings.

133. Women in Scholarly Publishing (WISP)
MIT Press
55 Hayward Street
Cambridge, MA 02142
Founded 1979
250 members
Tel. 617 263-5642
President: Kate Torrey
WISP encourages educational and professional advancement for its members and for women in scholarly publishing. It facilitates the exchange of ideas and assistance and exists as a national organization through which its members can act in con-

cert on issues that affect their welfare. WISP has a strong political focus on issues that relate directly to women's salaries and benefits, career development options, and representation.

Periodicals
What's New with WISP. Quarterly newsletter.
WISP Directory of Freelancers.

Each year WISP holds a half-day workshop on education and training at its annual meeting.

WISP's Career Development Fund will reimburse members for costs related to professional seminars or workshops that will enhance and develop participants' careers.

Author Societies

Horatio Alger Society (1961)
Editor, *Newsboy*: Gilbert K. Westgard II
SW 5th Ct.
Boynton Beach, FL 33435

Sherwood Anderson Society (1975)
Editors, *The Winesburg Eagle*
Dept. of English
Virginia Polytechnic Inst. and State Univ.
Blacksburg, VA 24061
Members: 150

Margaret Atwood Society (1982)
President: Kathryn VanSpanckeren
Dept. of English
Univ. of Tampa
Tampa, FL 33606
Members: 110

Jane Austen Society of America (1979)
President: Eileen Sutherland
4169 Lions Ave.
North Vancouver, BC V7R 352, Canada
Members: 2,500

Baker Street Irregulars (1934)
Wiggins: Thomas L. Stix, Jr.
31 Pierson Ave.
Norwood, NJ 07648
Members: 275

Frank Baum — see **International Wizard of Oz Club**

Samuel Beckett Society (1977)
President: Linda Ben-Zvi
Dept. of English
Colorado State Univ.
Fort Collins, CO 80523
Members: 350

American Boccaccio Association
Secretary-Treasurer: Michael Sherberg
Romance Languages and Literatures
Washington Univ., Campus Box 1077
One Brookings Dr.
St. Louis, MO 63130-4899
Members: 100

Brecht Society of America (1985)
Secretary
59 New St.
Dover, DE 19901

International Brecht Society (1980)
Secretary-Treasurer: Ward B. Lewis
Dept. of Germanic and Slavic
   Languages
Univ. of Georgia
Athens, GA 30602
Members: 270

Byron Society, American Committee (1971)
Executive Director: Marsha Manns
259 New Jersey Ave.
Collingswood, NJ 08108
Members: 300

James Branch Cabell Society (1965)
Treasurer: Dorys Crow Grover
Hall of Languages
East Texas State Univ.
Commerce, TX 75428
Members: 250

Lewis Carroll Society of North America (1974)
Vice President: Ellen Luchinsky
617 Rockford Rd.
Silver Spring, MD 20902
Members: 350

Willa Cather Pioneer Memorial (1955)
Newsletter Editor: Mildred R. Bennett
326 N. Webster
Red Cloud, NE 68970

Cervantes Society of America (1981)
Secretary-Treasurer: Alison Weber
Dept. of Spanish
Univ. of Virginia
Charlottesville, VA 22903
Members: 260

New Chaucer Society (1978)
Director: C. K. Zacker
Center for Medieval and Renaissance
    Studies
Ohio State Univ.
Columbus, OH 43210
Members: 600

G. K. Chesterton Society (1974)
Editor, *The Chesterton Review*: Ian Boyd
St. Thomas More Coll.
1437 College Dr.
Saskatoon, SK S7N 0W6, Canada

Paul Claudel Society
President: Philip A. Fulvi
Dept. of French and Italian
Pace Univ.
New York, NY 10038

Samuel Taylor Coleridge—see
Wordsworth-Coleridge Association

Wilkie Collins Society (1980)
President: Kirk H. Beetz
1307 F St.
Davis, CA 95616-1101
Members: 100

Joseph Conrad Society of America
Secretary: David R. Smith
Dept. of English
California Inst. of Technology
Pasadena, CA 91125

James Fenimore Cooper Society
    (1989)
Secretary: Hugh MacDougall
32 Elm St.
Cooperstown, NY 13326

Dante Society of America (1881)
Secretary-Treasurer: Richard Lansing
Harvard Univ.
61 Kirkland St.
Cambridge, MA 02138
Members: 330

Dickens Society (1970)
Secretary-Treasurer: Barry V. Qualls
Dept. of English
Rutgers Univ., Murray Hall 121
New Brunswick, NJ 08903
Members: 500

John Donne Society (1985)
Executive Director: Eugene R. Cunnar
Dept. of English
New Mexico State Univ.
Las Cruces, NM 88003
Members: 200

Arthur Conan Doyle—see **Baker
    Street Irregulars**

T. S. Eliot Society (1980)
President: Grover Smith
5007 Waterman Blvd.
St. Louis, MO 63108
Members: 200

Ralph Waldo Emerson Society (1989)
Editor of Newsletter: Wesley T. Mott
Dept. of Humanities
Worcester Polytechnic Inst.
100 Institute Rd.
Worcester, MA 01609

Robert Frost Society (1973)
Secretary and Director: Earl J. Wilcox
Dept. of English
Winthrop Coll.
Rock Hill, SC 29733
Members: 130

**Asociacion Internacional de
    Galdosistas (International Galdos
    Association)** (1976)
President: Germán Gullón
Dept. of Spanish and Classics
Univ. of California
Davis, CA 95616
Members: 275

**Association des Amis d'André Gide,
    American Committee** (1968)
Elaine Cancalon (Florida State Univ.),
    Catharine Savage Brosman (Tulane
    Univ.), and David Keypour (Huron
    Coll. of Western Ontario)
Dept. of Modern Languages and
    Linguistics
Florida State Univ.
Tallahassee, FL 32306
Members: 1,500

Ellen Glasgow Society (1974)
Secretary-Treasurer: Beverly S. Baker
1004 Ridge Top Rd.
Richmond, VA 23229
Members: 170

Goethe Society of North America (1979)
Executive Secretary: Ehrhard Bahr
Dept. of German
Univ. of California
Los Angeles, CA 90024-1539
Members: 250

Nathaniel Hawthorne Society (1974)
Secretary-Treasurer: Arthur Monke
Hawthorne-Longfellow Library
Brunswick, ME 04011
Members: 334

Hemingway Society (1980)
President: Robert W. Lewis
Dept. of English
Box 8237, Univ. of North Dakota
Grand Forks, ND 58202-8237
Members: 350

International Hopkins Association (1979)
Editor, *Hopkins Quarterly*: Richard F. Giles
Language Studies
PO Box 2034, Mohawk Coll.
Hamilton, ON L8N 3T2, Canada
Members: 175

Langston Hughes Society (1981)
Secretary-Treasurer: Alice A. Deck
Dept. of English
Univ. of Illinois
Urbana, IL 61801
Members: 150

Zora Neale Hurston Society (1984)
President: Ruthe T. Sheffey
7126 Minna Rd.
Baltimore, MD 21207
Members: 250

Ibsen Society of America (1978)
President: Rolf Fjelde
Dekalb Hall 3
Pratt Inst.
Brooklyn, NY 11205
Members: 120

Henry James Society (1979)
Editor, *Henry James Review*: Daniel
  Mark Fogel
English Dept.
Louisiana State Univ.
Baton Rouge, LA 70803-5001
Members: 450

**Samuel Johnson Society of the
  Northwest**
K. J. Ericksen and R. H. Carnie
Dept. of English
Univ. of Calgary
Calgary, AB T2N 1N4, Canada

**International James Joyce
  Foundation** (1967)
President: Morris Beja
Dept. of English
Ohio State Univ.
Columbus, OH 43210
Members: 750

James Joyce Society (1940)
President: Sidney Feshbach
Gotham Book Mart Gallery
41 W. 47th St.
New York, NY 10036
Members: 300

Kafka Society of America (1975)
Executive Director: Maria Luise
  Caputo-Mayr
Dept. of German, AB 335
Temple Univ.
Philadelphia, PA 19122
Members: 400

Keats-Shelley Association of America
  (1948)
Treasurer and Executive Director:
  Donald H. Reiman
Room 226, New York Public Library
5th Ave. and 42nd St.
New York, NY 10018
Members: 300 individuals; 700
  institutions

**D. H. Lawrence Society of North
  America** (1975)
President: Judith Ruderman
Office of Continuing Education
Duke Univ.
Durham, NC 27708
Members: 200

Doris Lessing Society (1980)
Vice-President: Jean Pickering
3958 N. Carruth
Fresno, CA 93705
Members: 210

G. E. Lessing Society (1966)
Secretary-Treasurer: Richard E. Schade
Dept. of German
Univ. of Cincinnati
Cincinnati, OH 45221-0372
Members: 350

New York C. S. Lewis Society (1969)
Secretary: Clara Sarrocco
84-23 77th Ave.
Glendale, NY 11385
Members: 600

Miss Mapp Society (1985)
President for Life: Patrick O'Connor
c/o Warner Books
666 Fifth Ave.
New York, NY 10103
Members: 65

Marlowe Society (1976)
President: Matthew Proser
Dept. of English
Univ. of Connecticut
Storrs, CT 06268
Members: 150

Melville Society (1946)
Secretary-Treasurer: Donald Yannella
Dept. of English
Glassboro State Coll.
Glassboro, NJ 08028
Members: 650

Mencken Society (1974)
President: Arthur M. Gutman
PO Box 16218
Baltimore, MD 21210
Members: 300

Edna St. Vincent Millay Society
(1985)
Directors: Elizabeth Barnett and John
    J. Patton
Steepletop
Austerlitz, NY 12017

Milton Society of America (1952)
Secretary: Albert C. Labriola
English Dept.
Duquesne Univ.
Pittsburgh, PA 15282
Members: 501

Nancy Mitford Society (1986)
President: Patrick O'Connor
c/o Warner Books
666 5th Ave.
New York, NY 10103

**William Morris Society in the
    United States** (1934)
Secretary-Treasurer: Hartley Spatt
Dept. of English
State Univ. of New York Maritime Coll.
Bronx, NY 10465
Members: 1,615 worldwide

Vladimir Nabokov Society (1978)
Secretary: Stephen Parker
Dept. of Slavic Languages and Literatures
Univ. of Kansas
Lawrence, KS 66045
Members: 250

Frank Norris Society (1985)
Executive Vice President: Jesse S. Crisler
Communication and Language Arts Div.
Brigham Young Univ., Hawaii
Laie, HI 96762
Members: 75

Eugene O'Neill Society (1978)
President: Frederick C. Wilkins
Dept. of English
Suffolk Univ.
Boston, MA 02114
Members: 250

Pirandello Society of America (1958)
President: Anne Paolucci
Dept. of English
St. John's Univ.
Jamaica, NY 11439
Members: 500

Poe Studies Association (1973)
President: Glen Allan Omans
Dept. of English
Temple Univ.
Philadelphia, PA 19122
Members: 260

Powys Society of North America (1983)
Executive Secretary: Denis Lane
1 West Pl.
Chappaqua, NY 10514
Members: 175

Proust Research Association (1969)
Editor, *Proust Research Association Newsletter*: J. Theodore Johnson, Jr.
Dept. of French and Italian
Univ. of Kansas
Lawrence, KS 66045-2120
Members: 350

Friends of George Sand (1976)
President: Natalie Datloff
Hofstra Cultural Center
Hofstra Univ.
Hempstead, NY 11550
Members: 250

Sartre Society of North America (1974)
Chair of Executive Board: Thomas R. Flynn
Dept. of Philosophy
Emory Univ.
Atlanta, GA 30322
Members: 500

Shakespeare Association of America (1972)
Executive Secretary: Nancy Elizabeth Hodge
Box 6328, Sta. B
Vanderbilt Univ.
Nashville, TN 37235
Members: 812

New York Shakespeare Society (1983)
Secretary: Karen Hornick
Dept. of English
Columbia Univ.
New York, NY 10027
Members: 100

Bernard Shaw Society (1962)
Secretary: Douglas Laurie
201 E. 19th St., 2N
New York, NY 10003
Members: 200

Percy Bysse Shelley—see **Keats-Shelley Association of America**

Spenser Society (1976)
Secretary-Treasurer: John Ulreich, Jr.
Dept. of English
Univ. of Arizona
Tucson, AZ 85721

International John Steinbeck Society (1966)
President: Ted Hayashi
Dept. of English
Ball State Univ.
Muncie, IN 47306
Members: 660

Wallace Stevens Society (1976)
President: John N. Serio
Clarkson Univ.
Potsdam, NY 13676

Tennyson Society
President: Mark Samuels Lasner
1870 Wyoming Ave., NW
Washington, DC 20009

Thoreau Society (1941)
Secretary: Michael Meyer
Dept. of English
Univ. of Connecticut
Storrs, CT 06269
Members: 1,400

Vergilian Society of North America (1937)
Executive Secretary: Robert J. Rowland, Jr.
Dept. of Classics
Univ. of Maryland
College Park, MD 20742
Members: 1,500

Evelyn Waugh Society (1967)
President: Paul A. Doyle
English Dept.
Nassau Community Coll., State Univ. of New York
Garden City, NY 11530
Members: 208

Edith Wharton Society (1983)
Annette Zilversmit
Dept. of English
Long Island Univ.
Brooklyn, NY 11201
Members: 300

William Carlos Williams Society (1980)
President: Theodora Rapp Graham
Humanities Div.
Pennsylvania State Univ. at Harrisburg
Middletown, PA 17057
Members: 200

International Wizard of Oz Club (1957)
Editor, *Baum Bugle*: Michael Gessel
PO Box 748
Arlington, VA 22216
Members: 2,600

Thomas Wolfe Society (1980)
President: Morton I. Teicher
4275 Nautilus Dr.
Miami Beach, FL 33140
Members: 500

Virginia Woolf Society (1975)
Secretary-Treasurer: Karen L. Levenback
1545 18th St., NW
Washington, DC 20036
Members: 210

Wordsworth-Coleridge Association
President: David Simpson
Dept. of English
Univ. of Colorado
Boulder, CO 80309

**Société Internationale d'Etudes
  Yourcenariennes** (1987)
C. Frederick Farrell or Edith R. Farrell
Div. of the Humanities
Univ. of Minnesota, Morris
Morris, MN 56267
Members: 200

**The North American Marguerite
  Yourcenar Society/La Société
  Marguerite Yourcenar** (1988)
Edith R. Farrell
Div. of the Humanities
Univ. of Minnesota, Morris
Morris, MN 56267
Members: 30

Appendix:
Checklist of Abbreviations

An asterisk (*) marks the abbreviations of organizations that are used in the text but not listed in the *Guide*.

AAA	American Anthropological Association
AAACE	American Association for Adult and Continuing Education
AAAL	American Association for Applied Linguistics
AAALS	American Association of Australian Literary Studies
AAASS	American Association for the Advancement of Slavic Studies
AABS	Association for the Advancement of Baltic Studies
AAIE	Amerika Asocio de Instruistoj de Esperanto (see AATE)
AAPY	American Association of Professors of Yiddish
AAR	American Academy of Religion
AAS	American Antiquarian Society
AAS	Association for Asian Studies
AATA	American Association of Teachers of Arabic
AATE	American Association of Teachers of Esperanto
AATF	American Association of Teachers of French
AATG	American Association of Teachers of German
AATI	American Association of Teachers of Italian
AATSEEL	American Association of Teachers of Slavic and East European Languages
AATSP	American Association of Teachers of Spanish and Portuguese
AAUP	American Association of University Professors
AAUW	American Association of University Women
ACA	American Culture Association
ACA	Association for Communication Administration
ACCELS	American Council for Collaboration in Education and Language Study (see ACTR)
ACH	Association for Computers and the Humanities
ACIS	American Conference for Irish Studies
ACL	American Classical League
ACL	Association Canadienne de Linguistique (see CLA)
ACLA	American Comparative Literature Association
ACLS*	American Council of Learned Societies
ACTFL	American Council on the Teaching of Foreign Languages
ACTR	American Council of Teachers of Russian
ACUTE	Association of Canadian University Teachers of English
ADE	Association of Departments of English
ADFL	Association of Departments of Foreign Languages
ADS	American Dialect Society
AEA	American Economic Association
AFS	American Folklore Society
AHA	American Historical Association

AHCT	Association for Hispanic Classical Theater
AHEA	American Hungarian Educators' Association
AHSA	American Humor Studies Association
AIA	Archaeological Institute of America
AJHS	American Jewish Historical Society
ALA	African Literature Association
ALTA	American Literary Translators Association
AMS	American Musicological Society
ANS	American Name Society
APA	American Philological Association
APA	American Philosophical Association
APFUCC	Association des Professeurs de Français des Universités et Collèges du Canada
APSA	American Political Science Association
ASA	African Studies Association
ASA	American Society for Aesthetics
ASA	American Sociological Association
ASA	American Studies Association
ASAIL	Association for the Study of American Indian Literatures
ASALH	Association for the Study of Afro-American Life and History
ASE	American Society for Ethnohistory
ASECS	American Society for Eighteenth-Century Studies
ASG	American Society of Geolinguistics
ASI	American Society of Indexers
ASTR	American Society for Theatre Research
ATESL	Administrators and Teachers in English as a Second Language
ATJ	Association of Teachers of Japanese
ATTW	Association of Teachers of Technical Writing
BSA	Bibliographical Society of America
BSC	Bibliographical Society of Canada
CAA	College Art Association
CALICO	Computer Assisted Language Learning and Instruction Consortium
CAPN	Classical Association of the Pacific Northwest
CAS	Canadian Association of Slavists
CCCC	Conference on College Composition and Communication (see NCTE)
CCL	Conference on Christianity and Literature
CEA	College English Association
CEE	Conference on English Education (see NCTE)
ChLA	Children's Literature Association
CLA	Canadian Linguistic Association
CLA	College Language Association
CLTA	Chinese Language Teachers Association
CLOIS*	Council for Languages and Other International Studies
CNL	Council on National Literatures
CSSEDC	Conference for Secondary School English Department Chairpersons (see NCTE)

EHA	Economic History Association
ESAA	Esperanto Studies Association of America
GLCML	Gay and Lesbian Caucus for the Modern Languages
HSS	History of Science Society
IAS/NAB	International Arthurian Society, North American Branch
IRA	International Reading Association
ISGS	International Society for General Semantics
JNCL*	Joint National Committee for Languages
LASA	Latin American Studies Association
LSA	Linguistic Society of America
LYRICA	Lyrica Society for Word-Music Relations
MELUS	Society for the Study of Multi-Ethnic Literature of the United States
MESA	Middle East Studies Association of North America
MGSA	Modern Greek Studies Association
MHRA	Modern Humanities Research Association, American Branch
MLA	Modern Language Association of America
MLG	Marxist Literary Group
MMLA	Midwest Modern Language Association
NAES	National Association for Ethnic Studies
NAFSA	National Association for Foreign Student Affairs
NAPH	National Association of Professors of Hebrew
NCTE	National Council of Teachers of English
NEASECS	Northeast American Society for Eighteenth-Century Studies
NEMLA	Northeast Modern Language Association
NFMLTA*	National Federation of Modern Language Teachers Associations
NHA*	National Humanities Alliance
NWSA	National Women's Studies Association
OAH	Organization of American Historians
PAPC	Philological Association of the Pacific Coast
PCA	Popular Culture Association
PES	Philosophy of Education Society
PNCFL	Pacific Northwest Council of Foreign Languages
PSA	Poetry Society of America
RETS	Renaissance English Text Society
RMMLA	Rocky Mountain Modern Language Association
SAH	Society of Architectural Historians
SALA	South Asian Literary Association
SAMLA	South Atlantic Modern Language Association
SASS	Society for the Advancement of Scandinavian Study
SBC	Société Bibliographique du Canada (see BSC)
SBL	Society of Biblical Literature
SCA	Speech Communication Association
SCE	Society for Critical Exchange
SCMLA	South Central Modern Language Association
SE17	Southeast American Society for French Seventeenth-Century Studies
SEM	Society for Ethnomusicology

SFRA	Science Fiction Research Association
SGRABL	Society for German Renaissance and Baroque Literature
SHOT	Society for the History of Technology
SSML	Society for the Study of Midwestern Literature
SSNL	Society for the Study of Narrative Literature
SSSL	Society for the Study of Southern Literature
SUS	Society for Utopian Studies
TCSAA	Twentieth Century Spanish Association of America
TESOL	Teachers of English to Speakers of Other Languages
UAA	Urban Affairs Association
WIG	Women in German
WISP	Women in Scholarly Publishing

Subject Index

The numbers given to are the entry numbers for the listings of associations, not the page numbers. Author societies are not included in this index.